Practical Boat Handling

CHAPMAN

Practical Boat Handling

Gregory O. Jones

WITH DAVE KELLEY

HEARST BOOKS
A DIVISION OF STERLING PUBLISHING CO., INC.
NEW YORK

Produced by J.A. Ball Associates, Inc.
Jacqueline A. Ball, President

Illustrations by Matt Fisher
Design and Production: Adam B. Bohannon
Photo Research: Sandra Will

Photography Credits Page 2: Brian Palmer/iStockphoto; Page 8: Courtesy Viking Yachts; Page 12: Ziella Marie Chua/iStockphoto; Pages 24, 120, 132, 156: Sea Tow; Pages 38, 74, 100: © Royalty-Free/Corbis; Page 60: Terry Healy/iStockphoto; Page 81: Courtesy Viking Yachts; Page 86: Gerry Walden Photography/photographersdirect.com; Page 94: Courtesy Viking Yachts; Pages 106, 144: United States Coast Guard; Page 117: Robert Kyllo/iStockphoto; Pages 135, 141, 148, 151: Courtesy of West Marine; Page 146: Courtesy of firstaidpak.com;

Library of Congress Cataloging-in-Publication Data Available

10 9 8 7 6 5 4 3 2 1

Published by Hearst Books
A Division of Sterling Publishing Co., Inc.
387 Park Avenue South, New York, N.Y. 10016

CHAPMAN, CHAPMAN PILOTING, and Hearst Books are trademarks of Hearst Communications, Inc.

Distributed in Canada by Sterling Publishing
c/o Canadian Manda Group, 165 Dufferin Street
Toronto, Ontario, Canada M6K 3H6

Distributed in Australia by Capricorn Link (Australia) Pty. Ltd.
P.O. Box 704, Windsor, NSW 2756 Australia

For information about custom editions, special sales, premium and corporate purchases, please contact Sterling Special Sales Department at 800-805-5489 or specialsales@sterlingpub.com.

Manufactured in China
Sterling ISBN 13: 978-1-58816-385-1
      ISBN 10: 1-58816-385-7

CONTENTS

Practical
Boat Handling

CHAPTER 1

INTRODUCTION

S o you've bought that new boat. There it is, all bright and shiny. You've got a collection of cleaners, waxes, and polishes to keep it in great shape. You can't wait to sit down and read the owner's manual beginning to end.

But what about actually driving the thing?

If you're a little intimidated, don't worry. That's how all boat owners feel the first time they pull out onto the lake or the harbor. While that's a safer emotion than overconfidence, anyone can learn to handle a boat with the ease and skill of a professional. It won't happen overnight; in fact, any sailor worthy of the name will tell you that you will never learn everything. That's part of the challenge and enjoyment of owning a boat.

Before we get any further, let's define "boat" as it will be used in this book. The advice on boat handling here applies to boats powered by engines. That includes not only powerboats but sailboats operating under engine power. It does not include sailboats operating under sail power, which would constitute a separate book. When advice does not apply to both powered sailboats and powerboats, it will be noted.

Under power, all boats are, basically, easy to handle. Things happen slowly. You're not going down the interstate at 65 miles an hour. You'll never have a blowout. There won't be anything to compare with those lines of traffic at rush hour. After all, you bought a boat because you wanted the freedom of the open water. The ability to set your own course, to your own destination.

In many ways, handling a boat under power is like driving a car. The throttle makes it go faster, and the wheel or rudder steers it. It has a transmission that shifts into forward, neutral, and reverse. Ahh, but the brakes… well, there aren't any brakes on a boat. However, you'll soon discover that a boat slows down pretty quickly when you back off the throttle, although you won't come to a complete stop this way. At slow speeds, the water resistance—the friction of the water against the hull—is minimal. You will notice this when you are coming into a dock or up to a mooring.

And when you're going slowly, you do have brakes of a sort. They're called "reverse." While you can't put the transmission into reverse at full power, you can, and should, use reverse to maneuver the boat at slow speeds. We will cover this in full detail in Chapters 4, 5, and 7.

Probably the most dangerous point in a skipper's learning curve is halfway through that first summer. That's about the time you think you've got it down. The boat usually reacts the way you want it to. You can pull up to the fuel dock without any unnecessary drama. Your launch technique is good enough so that the spectators have lost interest, and you can't remember the last time you messed up driving your boat onto the trailer.

That's when you have to keep in mind that learning to be a safe, competent boat operator is a lifetime job. While the learning curve gets less steep after you've been at it a few years, it is never flat. There's *always* more to learn.

One lesson here is to make sure the dock lines are stowed. Another is to make sure you and your crew go over everything on the boat before you shove off. But the biggest lesson is: Don't get over-confident. Good skippers pay attention to every detail. Little mistakes can add up to one big problem.

For the first few times you go out, take things easy. Go to an empty patch of water and practice turning, backing up, and holding the boat in position, using the engine and the rudder. See how long it takes the boat to slow down, and then see how long it takes to come to a stop when you are in neutral. Find out what the turning radius is, and then compare the circle when you turn to port or starboard. (It won't be the same, and we discuss the reasons for this in chapters 2 and 8.)

Bring along some small wood chips to drop in the water. Practice "docking" alongside the chips. Back up to one and see how straight you can go. Drop another one to come up to while going forward and then turn around it.

When you're feeling more confident, take the boat out when there's some chop, with enough wind to pick up the waves but not enough to make whitecaps. Drive the boat into the waves at a slow speed. Turn to cross the waves, and notice the difference in how the boat reacts. File the information away. There will come a time when things are a little hairy, and you'll be glad for the experience under calmer conditions. We cover boat handling in severe weather conditions in Chapters 10, 11, and 12; and while the main lesson is to avoid heavy weather whenever possible, a competent skipper should be prepared for any eventuality.

You will make mistakes; that's part of learning. You will scrape some gel coat at the dock. You will run aground. But if you take your boating seriously and learn from your mistakes, you will become a skilled boat handler. You can't learn it all from a book, but this book is a good place to start. The things you will learn as you go through this book all require practice. So there is homework—but it's the assignment of your dreams. Your homework is to go boating.

♟ Famous Flubs ☰

Terry is a professional mariner, the skipper of a tug that pushes strings of barges up and down the big rivers. He knows the Mississippi, the Missouri, and the Ohio. He's maneuvered his barges into locks with inches to spare on either side. But it was his first year of owning a 34-foot Bertram when, as he put it, "I learned about boats."

"I'd always wanted a bigger boat," he said. "I had a 23-foot bowrider, but I wanted something a little bigger for the family. And I wanted something my buddies and I could take out fishing in the Gulf. I got tired of seeing the big guys come back in with serious fish, but I didn't feel comfortable about taking the little boat out there."

On the way to the Gulf from his marina, near Lake Pontchartrain, Terry recalls: "We pulled up to the fuel dock and topped off the tanks, got ice, made sure everything was stowed all shipshape and headed out. At the end of the docks there was another boat going by, a commercial fishing boat, and I backed off to let him pass. We were nearly dead in the water and I gave it a little reverse to hold our position. There was some tide running and I wanted to make sure we didn't get in his way. I felt like it was piece of cake, compared to the tug."

Then he got his wake-up call. "Suddenly the engine just stopped. I was in gear, just starting to back down, and there was nothing. I hit the starter button, thinking the engine had just died for some reason, and all I heard was the solenoid on the starter click. The engine wouldn't turn over and now we were drifting out into the channel. I put it in neutral and the engine started, but when I put it in reverse, it died. Just like that. Instant."

He got on his VHF radio and told the fishing boat skipper he had no control and was drifting. The fishing boat cleared Terry's boat. Terry asked one of his crew to go to the bow and release the anchor.

"How do I do that?" asked his buddy. Then Terry realized he hadn't briefed the crew on the boat's systems. Drifting into the channel, he called the marina, hoping they would have a boat that could take him in tow. Within a few minutes—"It seemed like an hour," said Terry—a Sea-Tow boat showed up, threw him a towline and brought him back to the dock.

At the dock, he soon found the problem. "When we left the dock, I hadn't checked to make sure that all the lines were in. The stern dock line had just been laid down on the gunwale. It fell into the water and was fine as long as we were going ahead, but we backed right over it and wrapped it into the prop. I should have checked it, should have briefed everybody on what to do, but we were just in a hurry. I've pulled into and out of thousands of docks, but this time I just forgot."

It took a diver nearly an hour to cut the line loose. No harm was done and they got their fishing trip in, "but I'm glad we didn't jam that prop when were 10 miles out," Terry said. "I guess you never quit learning."⬤

CHAPTER TWO

THE BASICS

What makes a powered boat different from, say, a rowboat? The engine, of course. Wind and water currents move every boat, but the engine is the only thing the operator can control. How you operate that engine and steer your boat are the essentials of boat handling.

There are three basic classes of propeller-driven powerboats, and steering is accomplished differently depending on the class. A powerboat with an inboard engine is usually steered by its rudder, a flat, board-like object that pivots and produces resistance, causing the boat to move in the desired direction. If the rudder pivots to the right, the stern moves left and the bow moves right. The boat follows the bow and makes a right (or starboard) turn.

A boat with two engines and two props usually has two rudders. You can steer a twin-prop boat by using either the engines or the rudders. For maneuvering at slow speeds, putting one engine in reverse and the other forward will make a twin-engine boat turn very efficiently, nearly in its own length. At higher speeds, twin rudders steer just like single rudders.

The reason twin prop boats have twin rudders is that a rudder works better if it has its own prop in front of it. The water pushed by the propeller, the "prop wash," gives added force to the turning effect of the rudder. Because the prop wash does not hit the rudder when going in reverse, a boat doesn't steer as well when reversing. (Prop *wash* is a factor with both single- and twin-engine boats, but the effect of prop *walk*, discussed further in Chapters 3 and 8, is only a factor with single-prop boats.)

Powerboats with outboard motors steer by turning the motor and its attached propeller. If your boat has a wheel, and you turn it to the right, the motor will rotate to the right. The push of the propeller moves the stern left and the bow right. If your boat has an outboard but no wheel, the tiller handle is what rotates the motor and provides the turning force. *However, there's an important difference: with a tiller-steered outboard, you move the tiller to the left to make a right turn.*

Stern drives are a combination of inboard engine and outboard drive units that look very much like outboard motors. The engine is connected to the stern drive and the propeller with a flexible drive shaft. When you turn the wheel, the stern drive pivots, steering the boat just as though it was an outboard. With twin outboards or stern drives, you still have the advantages of an inboard twin-engine unit for maneuverability—plus you can still get home if one engine quits.

We've said that driving a boat is easier in some ways than driving a car. But in some ways it's harder. For one thing, a car follows its steering wheels when it turns. When a boat turns, it pivots at a point near its center, whether it's moving forward or backward. If you pull out of a curbside parking place, you don't have to worry that the rear wheels will hit the curb. But a boat tied up alongside a dock will bump its stern if you just turn the wheel and try to motor away. You have to maneuver.

Alternating between forward and reverse is an excellent strategy for close-quarters maneuvering. The prop will do much of the work, and giving short bursts of throttle will be more effective than keeping the engine at an idle. Never forget: At slow speeds, reverse equals brakes.

Another strategy when moving forward, or with the transmission in forward and the boat not moving, is to give the throttle short bursts. That will produce prop wash, which will hit against the rudder and move the stern sideways. However, this effect is nearly non-existent in reverse. When backing down the rudder only works when the boat is moving.

Another key car-boat difference: A boat's transmission is much simpler than a car's. There is only forward, neutral, and reverse. If you apply too much gas when accelerating, the prop will spin in the water, producing turbulence but not much drive. The "gear ratio" of a boat engine is determined by the propeller's "pitch." (That topic will be thoroughly covered in chapter 3.)

The last big difference between driving a car and a boat is that out on the water, there are no roads and few "street" signs. You have to navigate your boat to your destination, and that requires a new set of skills. There are a number of good books that deal with navigating a small boat. We also recommend you investigate the courses offered by the U.S. Power Squadrons, a volunteer organization dedicated to boating education. Yacht clubs often sponsor classes or workshops in navigation, maintenance, and even boat handling.

CHAPTER 3

PROPELLERS

P ropellers are the link between your engine and the water. Their style, size, material, and design have a considerable influence on your boat's performance and handling.

Propellers are measured by their *size* and *pitch*. You will find those measurements stamped onto the prop, usually near the hub. Look for two sets of numbers separated by an "x," as in "14 x 20" or "15 x 17." The first number is the propeller's diameter in inches. It will be easier to calculate, especially if you have a three-, four-, or five-blade prop, by measuring any blade from the tip to the center of the hub and multiplying that number by two.

To visualize pitch, imagine the propeller moving through a solid medium, "screwing" its way through the medium. The distance the propeller would go in one revolution is the pitch. In practice, of course, a boat with a 20-inch pitch prop won't go 20 inches per revolution because of the slippage in the water. Typically, a prop will have 10- to 15-percent of slip, so a prop with a 20-inch pitch will actually move forward something like 18 inches per revolution.

You can in effect "change gears" by installing a prop with a different pitch; however, for reasons we will explore later, you won't necessarily add 20 miles an hour to your boat's speed just by installing a prop with a bigger pitch. There are

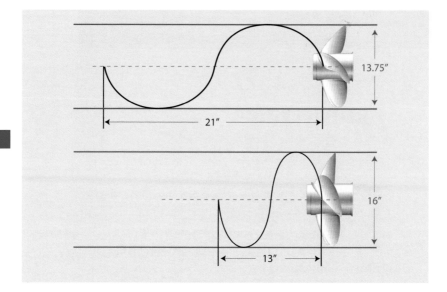

Diameter is the distance across the circle made by the blade tips as the propeller rotates. Pitch is the distance a propeller would advance in one rotation in a solid substance. These two propellers are of different diameter and pitch.

boats with variable pitch propellers, adjusted with a control in the cockpit or wheelhouse, but nearly all recreational powerboats have fixed-pitch props. Selecting the right pitch in the first place is vital. With the wrong propeller, you won't go as fast as you should. You won't have the power you need.

Besides diameter and pitch, the number of blades is also important. Propellers come with two to five or more blades, but most recreational powerboats have no more than four blades per propeller.

Props are designed to rotate in a specific direction. In addition to the numbers indicating the diameter and pitch, there may be the letters "RH" or "LH" stamped on the hub, for right-hand or left-hand rotation when moving forward.

A right-hand prop rotates clockwise (when viewed from directly astern) and a left-hand prop rotates counter-clockwise. Nearly all single-engine boats use right-hand props.

Single-engine boats have a tendency to move the stern in the opposite direction of the prop's rotation when going forward. This is called "prop walk." It is most noticeable at slow speeds. A right-hand rotation, single-engine boat set at idle with no one touching the wheel will at first make a slow turn to port as torque moves the stern counterclockwise to starboard, and then to starboard as prop wash acts on the rudder.

In twin-engine boats, the props will turn in opposite directions. That is, one prop will have a right-hand rotation and the other a left-hand rotation. This cancels out the effects of prop walk and is another reason why many boaters choose twin engine rigs.There is one single-engine rig that avoids prop walk: the "counter-rotating" drive. This is a drive unit on outboards or stern drives with two propellers on the same drive, in line with each other but rotating in opposite directions. The benefits are freedom from prop walk and greater efficiency, but with added complexity in the drive unit due to the gear train.

Propeller designers like to talk about "coverage," although you won't see this term on a propeller specification sheet. The easiest way to understand coverage is to imagine looking at a propeller with blades so wide that you can't see any space between them. That would be a prop with 100 percent coverage. Airplane propellers have a small percentage of coverage. The propellers of an ordinary household electric fan have a fairly high percentage of coverage.

The greater the coverage, the more water will be moved as the prop rotates. However, there are limits. A two-blade prop can only have a certain amount of coverage. You can't have a blade that is so wide that it fills half of the prop's rotating area. Added blades can each be smaller, but they still result in a high total percentage of coverage.

The number of blades also affects what is known as "blade loading." With two blades, each blade is stressed with half of the force needed to move the boat. Put on a three-bladed prop and the blade load is a third of the total force, and so on.

If you put too much load on a prop, it will spin in the water without producing drive, much like spinning your car's wheels in sand. "Cavitation" is the name given to the result of a prop spinning too fast or being supplied with more power than it can absorb (and use to propel the boat). What actually happens is that areas of low pressure are formed on the prop, usually beginning at the leading edge. When the pressure becomes low enough that the water will vaporize at its ambient temperature, it begins to boil. A cavitating prop produces bubbles of low-pressure water vapor and turbulence in the water surrounding the prop. This violent reaction, especially when the bubbles collapse, can accelerate the wear of the prop, causing pits and corrosion. The simplest way to reduce blade loading, then, is to increase either the size or the number of blades.

"Ventilation" is another result of putting too much power to a prop. It is often confused with cavitation. Ventilation is simply the result of the prop pulling in surface air or exhaust gas. This can happen in a sharp turn, as a result of wave action, or if the drive unit is up out of the water.

The number of blades has a direct relation to efficiency. If you have a two-blade prop on your outboard or stern drive, you can put more of the engine's power into the water (and thus into moving your boat) by switching over to a three-blade. If you have a three-blade prop, go up to a four-blade prop, and so on. Your new four-blade prop will "come out of the hole" faster and plane quicker. It may even plane at somewhat slower speeds, although planing speed is more directly related to hull shape than it is propeller design. Because the four blades will be able to put more power into the water, the boat will punch through heavy seas better than with three blades. But even in the midrange, a four-blade prop will be slightly faster than a three-blade.

Blade shape is also important. Look closely at any propeller blade and you will see that the blade's angle and shape are different at the hub and at the tip. The speed of the tip of a propeller blade is much faster than the speed next to the hub. The tip has to pass through the full circumference of the propeller, but the circumference of a circle an inch out from the hub is much smaller.

Some propellers are "cupped," with the trailing edge of the blades, especially near the tips, made with a slightly greater angle, as though that part had a higher pitch. The net effect is less slippage; that is, the distance a boat moves through the water with one revolution of the prop may be closer to the actual pitch than with a non-cupped prop.

The diameter of a propeller is also important. If you want to move a lot of water, you need a big propeller. A small propeller rotating very fast won't produce the same driving force as a big propeller turning slower. However, considerations such as blade loading, ventilation and cavitation force practical limits on how much you can get from a propeller of any size. The location of the propeller and the proximity of the hull or parts of the drive unit also impose practical limits on the maximum size of the prop. So the range of prop diameters is fairly limited.

This leaves pitch as the main variable. Here there is a wide range of choices. For most outboards or stern drives, the choice will be three- or four-blade props, except in the smaller outboard motors that come with two-blade props. Pitch determines your boat's performance, across the board, from acceleration to top speed to fuel burn rate. The selection of your propeller's pitch is entirely dependent upon what you want to do with your boat.

Let's look at an example. Take two identical 150-horse-power outboard motors. One will be used on a 24-foot bow rider owned by a family who spends weekends waterskiing and pulling the kids on water toys. Their favorite place to water ski is 15 miles from the launching ramp, and they're always in a hurry to get there.

The other motor will be used on a 26-foot pontoon boat whose owners like to entertain onboard and sometimes use the boat as a fishing platform. The pontoon boat will never see speeds over 20 knots. However, there could be a dozen people on board, plus food and beverages for the day.

The first family needs a prop with a high pitch, one that moves the boat through the water efficiently at high speeds. The pontoon boat family requires a prop with a low pitch. Both engines will be capable of operating at their maximum rpm, but the water skiers will be moving along at 40 knots or more, and the pontooners will be very comfortable at 18-20 knots, perhaps even slower.

If you put the water skiers' high-pitch prop on the pontooners' motor, you still wouldn't get the pontoon boat to do 40 knots. The water resistance of the pontoon boat's massive twin hulls would be so high that the engine wouldn't be able to turn the prop fast enough to produce 40 knots of speed. There might also be cavitation, with the prop churning in a froth of water but not delivering any speed.

If you put the pontooners' low-pitch prop on the water skiers' motor, you would get the 24-foot bow rider moving through the water with the engine buzzing away at maximum revs but only producing 20 knots of boat speed. It would be like driving in first gear all the time.

Since the selection of a prop is so critical, how do you know you have the right one for your boat and your style of boating? The simplest test is to get out on a clear stretch of water, on a day with little or no wind, and open the throttle. When the engine is running smoothly and will not rev any faster, check the engine tachometer. You want to find out if the engine will reach its maximum continuous operating rpm with the throttle wide-open. *(Note: Before you go out, find out what the rpm is by consulting the owner's manual or going to the engine manufacturer's website.)*

If your engine is under-propped (with a pitch that is too low) it won't be under sufficient load when at full throttle and the rpms will be excessive. With a low pitch, the boat will travel less distance with each rotation of the propeller. The boat will not go as fast as it could with the correct prop and the fuel burn rate will be higher.

If your engine is over-propped (with too high a pitch), you won't be able to get the engine up to maximum full throttle rpm. Running the engine at low rpms with high load can damage the engine as much as over-revving.

Why won't the boat keep going faster with a higher pitch prop? The resistance met by the boat as it goes faster increases geometrically. Increase the speed a little, the resistance increases a lot. At top speed, the engine cannot put enough power to the prop to get the boat to go any faster.

The horsepower that an engine produces increases as the engine revs faster, right up to the red line, or maximum rated rpm. (The red line is so named because tachometers often have a red line at the maximum rpm.) At that point, the power output falls of dramatically. You can damage an engine, even destroy it, by exceeding the maximum rpm. Most engines have a maximum continuous rpm, and this number generally is somewhere below the red line. The maximum continuous rpm should occur at the maximum desired (or designed) speed.

If the boat won't go as fast as you want with a given engine/prop combo, you can either put on a higher-pitched prop or a bigger engine. As we have noted, if you put a prop that is pitched too high for the engine's horsepower, the engine won't get up to its maximum sustained rpm range. The only choice is to get a bigger engine. That, too, has its limits. All boats are rated for the maximum engine size you can safely use. You can't turn a 14-foot bass boat into 100-mph race boat simply by sticking a 250-hp outboard on it.

Generally speaking, reducing the pitch by one inch—for example, going from a 14 x 16 prop to a 14 x 15 prop—will give you another 200 rpm. The same calculation works in the other direction, of course. If the engine is over-revving by, say, 400 rpm, increase the pitch by two inches.

Changing from a three-blade to a four-blade prop can also change the pitch to what you need. All other things remaining the same, switching to a four-blade will reduce your rpm by as much as 100 at wide-open throttle. You may find you get greater speed from your boat by going down an inch in pitch because the engine can rev more freely.

But the relationship between pitch and speed isn't absolute. Just as you can't turn a 14-foot bass boat into a racer by slapping a huge engine on it, neither can you get more speed by putting a high-pitched prop on it.

If you have a diesel engine, you can get a very good idea as to whether the prop is pitched correctly by observing the exhaust smoke. If the engine puts out a lot of black smoke when wide-open, you may have a propeller with too much pitch. The engine isn't turning over fast enough to burn the fuel being injected. The unburned fuel is coming out as black smoke. If the engine is revving too fast at wide-open throttle, then your boat has a prop that is pitched too low.

Some boaters keep several props on hand to tailor or "tune" the boat for that day's use. They put on a lower-pitched prop if they're going to pull water skiers, for maximum acceleration. They use a higher-pitched prop if they're going to be in a fishing tournament, and they want to move from one spot to another quickly.

The features of props to consider go beyond pitch and size. Props can be made of a number of metals, and there are now plastic, or composite, props on the market. Your choice of prop material will affect the price, how easily the prop can be repaired, its weight and the amount of blade flex. (All blades flex. The benefit of flex is that it can limit damage when you run aground. But excessive flex will limit how much power the propeller can transmit from the engine to the water.)

The most common propeller material is aluminum. Props made of aluminum are lighter in weight than stainless steel or bronze props and are relatively easy to repair. But you'll find, everything on a boat is a trade-off. Aluminum is more subject to damage from cavitation and electrolysis than stainless, bronze or composite. Aluminum props are rarely seen on boats with inboard engines, other than those with stern drives.

Stainless steel props are sturdy, long-lived—and expensive. They deliver high performance, especially on boats that put heavy loads on the prop, such as ski boats or off-shore fishing boats. Repairs can be difficult—translation, expensive—but a good stainless steel prop will generally last longer than an aluminum one. It will be more resistant

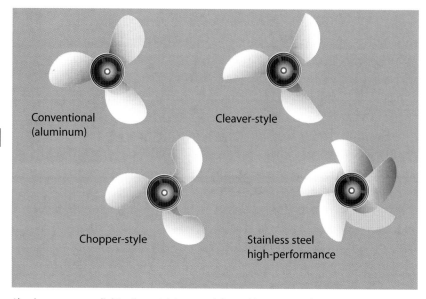

Aluminum props are lighter than stainless steel, but subject to more damage. Cleaver-style surfacing props are designed for stern drives and outboards. Chopper-style props are for sport boats at high speeds.

to minor damage from floating debris than aluminum or composite props. But like aluminum props, stainless steel ones are rarely used by boats with inboard engines.

Bronze is a traditional material for propellers. You can get bronze props for nearly any application, whether inboards, stern drives or outboards. Bronze is relatively easy to repair and provides good performance and long life, with very little flex in the blades. Bronze is also expensive, on a par with stainless steel. But it's easier to repair.

Composite props suitable for bigger engines are relatively new on the scene, but they provide a viable option for many boaters. They are relatively inexpensive; they are the lightest in weight; they're immune to electrolysis. Some types can be repaired by replacing individual blades through an operation so simple you can carry a spare blade for that purpose. Another attractive feature of some composite propellers is that you can afford to change their pitch, either by adjusting the angle of the blades on the hub or by replacing the blades.

At least one company makes composite props with an integral "hoop," or "ring" around the blades. The ring connects the blades, and covers the tips, which can greatly reduce damage if the prop strikes something. The ring reduces prop walk as well.

Composite props don't have the high-end, big-engine performance characteristics of metal props, but the development is ongoing. Some day metal props might be thought of as quaint remnants of an earlier era. For now, aluminum, bronze, or stainless steel props provide the greatest strength and performance, with composites having the edge in cost and ease of repair.

Your boat, whether new or used, inboard, stern drive or outboard, will almost certainly come with a propeller, but even on a new boat the included prop will most likely be a compromise prop—one that will serve all purposes acceptably. Do some testing to determine if the prop really suits your boat and your pattern of use. Changing your prop is fairly easy, but having a tool called a propeller puller will make the job easier. These come in several different varieties. Ask your local chandlery for advice. Many boaters carry a spare prop to get them home if they damage the one on their engine. If you replace or upgrade your prop, hang on to the old one if it is still working. Even if it's the "wrong" prop it will work in a pinch to get you home.

Props rarely die of old age. Navigate with care and you won't have to replace a prop until you want to change your boat's performance.

CHAPTER 4

LAUNCHING AND RETRIEVING

Show of "hands": Which boater wouldn't like to have a private, covered slip at a first-class marina? Well, the reality is that most recreational boaters tow their craft to and from the water. That's why launching—getting the boat off the trailer—and retrieving—getting the boat back on the trailer—are two absolutely required boat handling skills. Adding to their importance is the fact that launching and retrieving are the skills boaters will most often be showing off to a critical, impatient group of people: the other boaters waiting to use the launching ramp.

It would stand to reason that the skills we use most often and the skills we most often have to perform in public would be the ones we concentrate most on perfecting. In this case, not so. Too many recreational boaters think of launching and retrieving as necessary evils at best, and they cavalierly neglect to follow even the most basic rules of boat handling when around the launch ramp. Ramp Rage isn't quite as prevalent as its cousin, Road Rage, but sitting in too long a line at a crowded ramp, only to see the person ahead of you tie up the ramp for an hour, could have the same kind of effect.

There are two main rules to remember when launching and retrieving: Be Prepared, and Go Slowly. Virtually everything that can go wrong when launching or retrieving is a direct result of a lack of preparation or trying to rush.

Pre-launch Checklist: Things to Do Before Getting In Line to Launch

☐ Fill boat's tanks, both fuel and water.

☐ Check all engine fluid levels, fill if necessary.

☐ Attach battery cables if disconnected during storage, or turn battery switch to "ON" position.

☐ Check steering function. Turn wheel to be sure that drive unit/rudder is operational.

☐ Make sure registration is valid and numbers are intact and visible.

☐ Insert and secure drain plug.

☐ Transfer all gear from tow vehicle to boat, stow and secure all gear.

☐ Make sure there is at least one PFD on board for every passenger.

☐ Remove and stow all coverings.

☐ Double-check drain plug installation. (Even on new boats, drain plugs might not be installed)

Being prepared means being totally prepared to launch or retrieve before getting into the launching queue, not being "ready to get ready." If necessary, create a checklist (see sidebar for an example) so that you can make sure that nothing is overlooked.

Going slowly means taking a few extra seconds to do the job right the first time so you won't have to repeat the process. A crew will make launching much easier, but in good weather a solo boater who is prepared and goes slowly can easily accomplish a safe launch.

Launching in Calm Conditions

Here are the steps to follow in calm weather:

1 Start close to the edge—it doesn't matter which side—of the launch ramp.

2 Drive forward slowly and make a big, arcing turn as near the water as possible so that you finish with your vehicle on the opposite edge of the ramp, facing away from the water. This will make it easier to back the boat/trailer tandem. The less you have to steer while backing the boat/trailer tandem, the better. Pull far enough forward from the water to allow maneuvering room, however.

3 Set the parking brake, get out, and check to make sure the boat's drain plug is secured, the drive unit is up (and the support bracket, if there is one, is removed), the trailer's lights have been unplugged, and all the tie downs except the bow strap have been released. This is also a good time to start the bilge blower.

4 Once back in the tow vehicle, straighten its wheels, then put your hands at the *bottom* of the steering wheel. This hand position means that you don't have to remember counter-steering. If your hands are at the bottom of the steering wheel and you want the boat/trailer tandem to go left, for example, you simply move your hands to the left. Don't look over your right shoulder while backing up because the boat/trailer tandem will obstruct your view. Use your side mirrors to see where you're going, and back up very slowly.

5 Back the trailer into the water until the wheels are partially submerged. Avoid backing so far that the tow vehicle's

rear wheels reach the water line. That can compromise traction and create an unsafe condition.

6 Stop and set the tow vehicle's parking brake. At this point, the boat should be still resting on the trailer bunks but getting just a hint of flotation.

7 To check the flotation, loosen the bow strap and push the boat toward the back of the trailer, as though you were going to push it completely off the trailer. If you can easily push the boat back a few inches, you have enough flotation. If you can't move the boat at all, return to the tow vehicle and back up another foot or so. Test the flotation until you've reached the magic point of easy flotation. Loosen

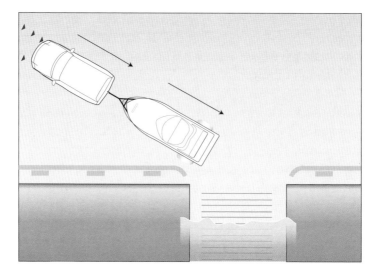

Approach in reverse when launching. Remember that the trailer backs in the opposite direction of the car.

the bow strap and disconnect it from the boat. The boat shouldn't be tied to the trailer at all.

8 Climb aboard, deploy boat fenders, and prepare a dock line so you can quickly secure the boat to the dock after launching. Start the engine, leaving the drive unit trimmed as high as possible. Look behind you to make sure the area is clear. Put the throttle in reverse and back the boat off the trailer as slowly as possible.

9 Pull around and dock the boat so the launch area will be clear when you move the tow vehicle and trailer. Secure the boat to the dock, then move the tow vehicle and trailer to a designated parking area. Even if it's a Tuesday afternoon in

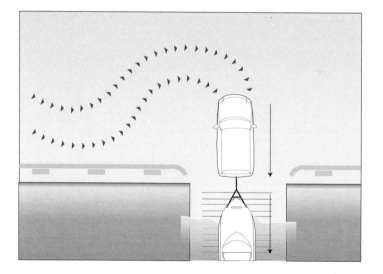

Straighten the car wheels to follow the trailer as it backs down the ramp.

January, with sleet coming down and small craft warnings in full effect, move the tow vehicle and trailer immediately. If you used the ramp, you can be sure someone else will want to use it as well.

If the weather is less than optimal, especially if there are winds, consider postponing the outing. Winds are the biggest concern when launching, since you're in very tight quarters with little room to maneuver and little opportunity to use throttle to counter the winds' effects. The boat can easily be pushed heavily into the trailer (and in extreme cases all the way into the tow vehicle) by a tailwind or waves, and a headwind can push the boat off the trailer before you're able to climb aboard after releasing the bow strap. *(Don't think even for a second about trying to reach over the bow and release the bow strap from on board the boat. This is very dangerous.)* Crosswinds can blow the boat off the trailer and into a dock, another boat, or even another trailer.

Launching in Windy Conditions

In windy conditions, the assistance of a crewmember is a necessity, as is a dock near the launch ramp. The safest method for launching in windy conditions is to follow the same procedures as for clear weather, up until the point where the trailer wheels are partially submerged and the boat is resting lightly on the trailer bunks (Step 5). Instead of releasing the bow strap and then climbing aboard, first deploy boat fenders and secure two dock lines to the boat, one at the bow and one at the transom. Have your crew member hold the stern line while you handle the bow line. You should both have good footing and stay completely out of the water.

As you loosen and release the bow strap, the crewmember should keep the stern line taut to keep the boat from drifting off the trailer too soon. Using the dock lines like reins on a team of horses, you and your crew member can safely guide the boat off the trailer and to a safe position on the dock from which you'll be able to push off without too much trouble. Secure the boat to the dock, move the tow vehicle and trailer to a designated parking spot, and you're ready to shove off.

Sometimes launching can be tricky, even in perfect weather, due to the presence of currents that will try to pull the boat one way or the other as soon as you get off the trailer. As a general rule, launch ramps are designed to avoid currents, but that's not always possible.

When Launching into a Crosscurrent

When launching into a crosscurrent, if you have a crewmember who can assist, use the method described above for windy conditions. If you're going it alone and there's a dock that extends from the launch ramp, back the trailer so the boat is as near the dock as possible. Before releasing the bow strap, deploy fenders to protect the boat from the dock and attach a bow line. Run the bow line through a dock cleat about amidships (if a dock cleat is not available, pass the line around a piling) so you can use it as a spring line. Release the bow strap and climb back aboard. Hold the spring line fairly taut, but not overly so, and bump the throttle gently and just for a split-second into reverse.

As the boat drifts off the trailer, use the spring line to pull the boat snug against the dock. You can now push or walk the boat to the end of the dock, where it can be safely secured while you park the tow vehicle and trailer.

If there's no dock that extends from the launch ramp, back the boat/trailer combo into the water as far upstream from any obstacles as possible. You'll need all the maneuvering space you can get. Follow the procedures for standard launching, but as soon as the boat is off the trailer, turn the steering wheel all the way "upstream" (opposite the direction the current is trying to push you) and apply strong reverse throttle. As you reverse, the engine should essentially hold its position while the current pushes the bow down river. That's the plan—to use the current to initiate a turn while you're reversing.

When you're a safe distance away from shore and any obstacles, turn the wheel all the way "downstream," then apply a burst of forward throttle. Don't apply forward throttle until the wheel has been fully turned, so you get the full benefits. Hold the turn and the throttle until the boat is headed safely away from shore, then straighten the wheel and back off the throttle. Now you're ready to return to the dock, where you can secure the boat until you've safely parked the tow vehicle and trailer.

Retrieving

It's sometimes said that in good conditions, retrieving is simply a matter of reversing the steps involved in launching. That's close, but not completely accurate.

The first step in retrieving is to return the boat to the launch area and secure it to the dock (for more on docking, see Chapter 5) until you can back the trailer into the water. It's very important that you keep the tow vehicle's rear wheels completely out of the water and on the driest pavement possible for maximum traction when you pull the boat/trailer combo out of the water. Set the parking brake and return to the boat.

One of the most common retrieving mistakes is to leave insufficient maneuvering space for the boat so you wind up approaching the trailer at a difficult angle. Give yourself plenty of room so that you can approach the trailer as straight-on as possible. When you're in position and are ready to approach the trailer, trim the drive unit up as much as possible so the propeller doesn't run aground.

The rule of thumb for retrieval in good weather is "the slower you go, the easier it is." Believe it or not, even coming in at idle speed can be too fast. *The key is to work the throttle delicately, bumping it into drive—and no further than idle speed—for just a split-second, just enough to maintain momentum and steering control, then dropping the throttle back to neutral so the boat glides forward gently until it comes to rest on the trailer's bunks.*

Once the boat has come to rest on the bunks, attach a bow line and hold on to it until you can secure the bow strap. Then winch the boat up onto the trailer until the bow is snugly fitted into the trailer's bow receptacle. Toss the bow line back on board and pull the tow vehicle and boat/trailer combo clear of the launch ramp, back to the designated parking area.

When you're parked out of everyone's way, reattach the trailer lights, secure any gear inside the boat (and move any gear necessary back into the tow vehicle), secure the boat to the trailer, and remove the drain plug so any accumulated water can drain out on the way home.

As with launching, currents can make retrieving challenging even on an otherwise perfect day. Back the trailer into the water as far downstream from any obstacles, including docks, as possible. Take the boat away from the dock, out into the current, and let it drift for a few seconds to get a feel for how strong the current is. When you're ready to approach the trailer, position the boat well upstream, but angled so it's pointing straight at the shore. This position will allow the current to push you strongly, so give yourself plenty of drifting room.

Gently bump the throttle, as you would in perfect conditions, turning the steering wheel "upstream" to keep the boat as perpendicular to the shore as possible. The trick—and it will take some practice to master—is to coordinate the boat's drift with the throttle bursts, while keeping the boat perpendicular to the shore, so that the final burst is delivered just as the boat aligns with the trailer so it can push the boat right up onto the bunks.

When dealing with currents, don't feel committed to the retrieval if it becomes obvious that things are going wrong. If you're going to have to fight your way upstream, even for just a few yards, to get the boat onto the trailer, back off, regroup and try again.

The most important thing is to be very deliberate in your maneuvering. Avoid a panicked rush, no matter how many times it takes you—even if the conditions have turned bad.

Retrieving with Wind

Of all the possible bad weather conditions, the easiest to handle is a strong headwind. This will require a bit more throttle action on your part, and you'll have to be a bit more hands-on with the steering, as the wind will try to push your bow one way or the other. In this situation, retrieve as you would in calm, clear weather, only with more aggressive throttle and steering application.

Retrieving with a following wind, or tailwind, is trickier. The boat's transom offers the wind a nice, large area to push against, and the contours of the shore around the launch ramp are tailor-made for creating following waves that will torment your approach to the trailer.

Successful retrieval with a following wind requires a steady hand on the steering wheel and a light touch on the throttle. For the most part, you'll let the wind push the boat toward and onto the trailer, using the throttle to provide the power needed to maintain steering control. Use short, controlled bursts of forward power to assist in steering, and short, strong bursts of reverse throttle to slow the boat as it nears the trailer.

In the shallow water around a launch ramp, even a moderate wind can whip up choppy waves or whitecaps. The waves will help the wind push your craft, but they can also cause your boat to bob up and down as you approach the trailer. If the wave takes control of the boat it could hit the trailer and break something. The key is more or less to match speed with the waves, keeping the forward portion of the hull in the trough between waves, especially in the critical final approach to the trailer. Don't get too aggressive with the throttle trying to overcome the waves, This will make the waves' bobbing effects worse and can lead to the boat smacking into the trailer.

When there's a following wind, be ready and willing to abort the retrieval attempt and start again if things aren't going exactly according to plan. Your margin for error is virtually nonexistent. The wind and waves can easily cause you to beach the vessel on the launch ramp (very bad) or overshoot the trailer (very, very bad).

Crosswinds are best handled in the same manner as crosscurrents, although a wind coming directly from port or starboard is somewhat rare. You'll almost always be dealing with quartering winds, where the wind is coming from two o'clock, four o'clock, eight o'clock, or ten o'clock (if twelve o'clock is directly in front of you and six o'clock is directly behind you). Since these winds will affect your boat and its handling just like a combination of, for example, a headwind and a crosscurrent, the way to deal with them is to combine the procedures for those conditions.

Let's say you're dealing with a quartering wind that's coming from two o'clock, or off the starboard bow. The wind will try to push you away from and to the left of the trailer you're trying to reach. Give yourself plenty of room to maneuver and begin your approach with the trailer well to port. Use short, light bursts of forward power and keep the steering wheel turned to starboard, as though you're trying to head the boat into the wind. You don't want to actually turn the boat into the wind, though. Your goal is to simply counter the wind, keeping the boat as perpendicular as possible to the shoreline. When you reach the trailer, no more than 10 feet or so away, you should be positioned so you can drive straight ahead and onto the bunks. Straighten the wheel and give a strong burst of forward power. This should drive you right up onto the trailer.

A quartering wind from eight o'clock, over the port transom, is a bit trickier. Again, begin the approach with plenty of maneuvering room. The wind will try and push the boat to the right of and past the trailer, so speed control is very important. Keep the steering wheel turned to port, to counter the wind, and give very small bursts of forward power only as needed to keep the boat at a 90-degree angle to shore so you'll be able to drive straight up and onto the trailer. Again, when the boat is within about 10 feet of the trailer, straighten the wheel and give a final, very small burst of forward power, letting the wind do most of the work of pushing the boat onto the trailer.

Once the boat is on the trailer, your actions should be

the same as in perfect weather. Attach a bow line so you can maintain contact with and control of the boat as you climb out and reattach the trailer's bow strap. Winch the boat up snugly, secure the other tie-downs, remove the drain plug, and clear the launch ramp so the next person can get his or her boat safely out of the water as well.

Famous Flubs

About the third or fourth time I came at the trailer and the boat slipped to the side, I got really mad." Art had just come back from his second day on the water in his 25-foot Bayliner. Unlike the previous day, there was enough wind blowing to complicate things and Art just couldn't get it right. "By the third time, there was a crowd along the launch ramp, and they were all giving me advice," said Art. "All I wanted to do was to be left alone to figure it out and get my boat onto the trailer," said Art. "After the fourth time I just told myself to tune out the noise. I motored up to the trailer, and it blew off again. But this time I paid attention to the wind and how I was steering. When I backed out again I sat for a minute to think about what the wind was doing and then I went in again."

His fifth try wasn't successful either, "but this time I was off on the other side. So when I tried again I 'split the difference' and used less steering and headed the boat more into the wind. I cut the engine at the right time and the boat just slid onto the trailer," said Art. "That felt good, and it was even better when I noticed that the gang on the dock was quiet." He smiled and added, "I almost hated to ruin their fun."

CHAPTER 5

DOCKING AND UNDOCKING

Docking and undocking are indispensable boat handling skills for even the most infrequent boater. Whether you are pulling alongside a gas dock or into a marina slip, the ability to safely dock your craft is one that you'll use almost every time you go out on the water.

Docking and undocking are somewhat analogous to parking a car or truck. There's the relatively simple and straightforward head-in method, the somewhat more difficult trick of reversing your vessel into place, and the not-as-tricky-as-it-seems parallel positioning. Of course, they are all a bit more difficult in a boat than in a car or truck. In a boat, you have to deal with possibly unfamiliar handling characteristics, wind, currents, and the inescapable lack of brakes, which means you have a much smaller margin for error.

There are so many variables involved when docking or undocking that every experience will be unique. That means you have to pay attention each and every time you dock. It also means that paying attention will be easier—you'll always have something a little different confronting you. But there are a few rules of thumb to make any docking or undocking easier.

First, *slow down.* Speed causes more problems than it

solves. Go slowly and give yourself time to think and act.

Second, *survey the situation*. Even if you're pulling back into the marina slip you've used for the past 25 years, as you make your approach you need to take a moment to make a detailed mental survey of the situation. Are you in a position to deal with boat traffic? Is there any factor of wind or current? How will you be positioning the boat: bow in, stern in or parallel? How much room do you have for maneuvering? Are there any dockhands available to assist if necessary? If you want to be successful, each of these factors must be taken into account as you plan and execute your approach.

Third, *be prepared*. Before you even begin your approach to a dock, you should have your lines ready and fenders deployed. You should have a plan for how you're going to handle the docking or undocking, and that plan should have a couple of options in case you misjudge something or conditions change. If you have passengers or crewmembers on board, they should know their tasks and be in position during the maneuver, or they should be safely out of the way. Caution all passengers aboard against using their bodies to fend off if contact with the dock or another vessel is imminent. If there are dockhands, you should have made visual contact with them and indicated your approach so they can be in position to assist.

Fourth, *be willing to try again*. There's no shame in admitting you were in an untenable position and having another go (think of it as claiming an unplayable lie and taking a drop if your golf ball comes to rest at the foot of a sleeping grizzly bear). Probably 95 percent of docking and undocking mishaps could be avoided if the captain would simply back off and start over instead of trying to salvage an effort. Invariably, by the time the captain realizes his boat is not in position to dock properly, he's quickly running out of time and space in which to maneuver, yet often he soldiers on, trying to force his boat to make difficult, if not impossible, adjustments. The inevitable bad outcome can range from harsh words between captain and crew to a collision with a dock or nearby vessel, or even bodily harm. The forces involved are considerable: Imagine a ton of weight concentrated on someone's foot caught between the boat and the dock.

Docking in Calm Conditions

The easiest of all dockings is when you have the option of pulling your boat bow-first into a marina slip when the winds and currents are all but nonexistent. If you're really lucky, your intended slip will be situated so that you can simply idle the boat straight in without as much as turning the steering wheel. However, more often you'll have to maneuver the boat into your slip after making your way along a row of slips, so even if wind and current aren't messing with you too much, you'll still have to do a little work with the wheel and throttle.

The most important thing to remember when docking in calm conditions is that less is more, especially when it comes to throttle use. Whenever power is needed, whether to initiate or stop a maneuver or to propel or stop the boat, use as little as possible, for the shortest time possible. You can always give another brief "bump" to continue or counter your movement, but you can never take an application of power back.

Since you're in a marina, you'll be idling toward your intended slip, keeping your boat in the center of the channel between slips. Many inexperienced boaters hug the row of slips opposite their intended slip, staying as far away as possible to give them what they think is maximum maneuvering room. But this is wrong. Boats don't turn the same way cars do, with the back following the front. All boats, power or sail, pivot around their center points, so at slow speeds they pivot rather than turn. A pivot from the far edge of your row will bring your stern too close to boats in the opposite slips. What you want is the widest possible turning arc in the center of the channel.

As you get within, say, 10 yards of your intended slip, keep the wheel pointed straight ahead and put the drive in neutral. Then use a brief "bump" of reverse gear and throttle to bring the boat nearly to a stop just before your intended slip. Even though boats pivot nearly exactly in place at low speeds, they travel a little bit, so you'll need this spatial cushion. If yours is a single outboard or stern drive boat, turn the wheel all the way *toward* your intended slip (i.e., if the slip is to port, turn the wheel hard to port). If your boat has an outboard motor with a tiller, push the tiller *away* from your intended slip.

With the wheel fully turned, apply a low-power burst of forward for just a split-second. This will initiate the pivot turn and propel the boat slightly forward, beginning to line it up with your intended slip. As the boat pivots, turn the wheel or pull the tiller all the way in the opposite direction, shift into reverse and apply another brief burst of throttle. This will accelerate the pivot.

As the boat aligns with the slip, center the wheel or the tiller and apply a brief, light burst of forward. This will stop the pivot and nudge the boat into the slip. When the bow gets within a few feet of the forward end of the dock, leave the wheel or tiller in the center position and apply a final, brief bump of reverse throttle to stop your momentum. Finally, deploy dock lines and secure your boat.

Reversing into slips is the preferred docking method of larger boats because it allows boarding and debarking via the transom or swim platform, as the bow and gunwales of these boats are often too high to allow safe boarding or debarking. Fortunately, these larger boats are often equipped with twin engines and drives, which greatly increase the boat's maneuverability and more than offset the handling difficulty that comes with the added size.

Transom-in Docking

Setting up for a transom-in docking in a single outboard or stern drive boat is similar to setting up for a bow-in docking. Idle toward your intended slip, keeping to the center of the channel. When you reach the slip before your intended slip, bump the drive into reverse just enough to stop your momentum. With the drive in neutral, turn the wheel all the way away from your intended slip (i.e., if your intended slip is to port, turn the wheel hard to starboard), as if you were going to dock bow-first in the slip opposite yours. If you're using a tiller, you'll push it all the way toward your intended slip. Start the pivot with a bump of forward. Turn the wheel or push the tiller in the opposite direction and bump reverse to stop the pivot when in line with the slip. Center the wheel or tiller and back into the slip, slowly.

If your boat has multiple engines and drives, including boats with inboard engines and drive trains, you have an advantage. Let's say your intended slip is to port. Your boat is essentially motionless in the center of the channel between rows of slips, with your intended slip—for the purposes of this example—directly to port. Put the drives in neutral and center the steering wheel, so that if you were to apply forward gear and throttle, the boat would go straight ahead. As odd as it may seem, from this point on you won't use the steering wheel at all.

With the throttles pulled all the way back to idle, simultaneously shift the port drive to forward and the starboard drive to reverse. Only if needed, apply a very light, very brief bit of throttle, making sure to apply as close to identical power as possible to each engine. This will essentially pivot the boat, albeit very slowly, on its axis. As the boat rotates, reverse the drive settings, so that now the port drive is

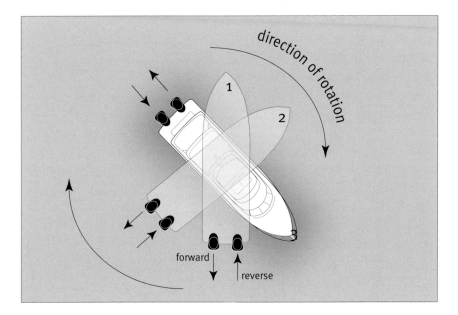

A twin-screw boat is easily turned in its own length by going forward on one engine with the other in reverse.

in reverse and the starboard drive is in forward to stop the boat's rotation when aligned with the slip. Now, with both throttles at idle, shift both drives to reverse. *Do not use the steering wheel.* The boat should now be reversing in a straight line, right into the slip. As the boat gets within a few feet of the dock, shift to neutral and then forward. Apply a bump of forward throttle to both engines simultaneously to stop the boat's momentum. Deploy dock lines and secure the boat.

Since you never use the steering wheel to maneuver in the above scenario, this is a technique that you should practice in a safe place until you get the hang of using only the drives and throttles to steer the boat. Find a secluded cove where you can spend time perfecting this close-quarter, no-steering-wheel maneuver. Practice with throttles at idle. When you become more comfortable with this docking technique, you can apply small bursts of power to enhance the maneuvers.

If you're going into a slip transom-in and have a single-screw boat with one inboard engine and right-hand propeller, you'll pull forward as you would for a bow-in docking, again bringing the boat to a stop in the center of the channel, next to your intended slip. With the gear in neutral—again, we're imagining the intended slip is to port—turn the steering wheel full to starboard, as if you were planning to pull into the slip directly opposite your intended slip. Apply a bump of forward gear and throttle, so the boat begins to pivot stern to port, bow to to starboard as the prop's discharge current hits the rudder. With wheel still to starboard, apply a bump of reverse gear and throttle. This will activate the opposite prop torque, and the stern will "walk," or swing, to port. This maneuver will actually speed up the pivot, so be ready to turn the steering wheel back to port and apply another bump of forward gear and throttle, if necessary, to stop the rotation.

At this point, you should be more or less in front of and aligned with your intended slip, so all that's left is to center the helm and reverse the boat in. Because the stern will again tend to walk to port, it may be necessary to apply a small amount of starboard rudder, to keep the boat moving straight back into the slip. It's highly recommended, however, that you deploy fenders and ready dock lines before you approach the slip. Getting a single-engine boat to reverse in even a generally straight line for a limited distance is quite difficult. Remember with a single-screw inboard with right-hand prop, it's always best to use a port-side dock when backing in. Prop torque makes docking starboard-side very challenging.

Docking alongside, as opposed to docking into, a slip is a maneuver all boaters have to perform with great frequency, even if they have a slip for their boat. The best analogy is to parallel parking in a car or truck: sometimes you'll get to park alongside an empty curb so there's plenty of room to just pull right up, and sometimes you'll have to perform a few precision dance steps in order to squeeze into a tight spot between two other vehicles.

In the best of circumstances, there will be plenty of dock space available so you can essentially "drive up" and dock without having to do much maneuvering at all. In this situation, approach the dock at an angle and pick a target spot where you're going to try and bring the bow to the dock. The more perpendicular your approach to the dock, the more delicate and difficult the maneuver will be, because you'll have a reduced margin of error.

Approach the dock slowly. In our experience, it's best to approach at less than idle speed if you can, using just enough bumps of forward throttle to keep the boat moving and under control. What you're going to do in this maneuver can be best described as skidding sideways to the dock. Newton's First Law of Motion (an object in motion will remain in motion unless acted upon by an outside force) applies to boats, so if you get the boat heading toward the dock, even if you turn the boat, its momentum will keep carrying it in the direction it was traveling. So what you'll be doing is setting the boat on a course for the intended docking spot, then "throwing it sideways" and letting it coast to a stop. Of course, the slower the boat is "coasting," the easier it is to alter its course and the gentler the meeting of dock and hull will be. So the goal is to approach the dock with enough speed to coast on in, but not so much that you coast in without 100 percent control.

As you approach the dock, mentally calculate your boat's size and speed so you can gauge the appropriate time to begin maneuvering. This will be different for every boat. Again, practice whenever you can find an empty dock so you can master your own boat's characteristics.

Because of the physics of propeller rotation, most single-engine inboards with right-hand prop experience some "portside prop walk" when the drive is in reverse, a situation where the stern seems to go perfectly sideways to its left instead of backwards. Instead of fighting this, use it to your advantage and dock port-side whenever possible. Here's how:

As the bow nears the dock, put the gear/throttle in neutral and turn the wheel hard to starboard. Then apply a gentle, brief bit of forward to start the boat pivoting in that direction. The shallower your approach angle, the closer you can be to the dock when you begin the pivot. If you're coming in very shallow, you might be able to get within a couple of feet of the dock before the pivot, while a 90-degree, head-on approach might require you to start the maneuver a boat's length or two away from the dock, so there will be enough room for the boat to rotate before reaching the dock.

Once the pivot has begun, put the gear/throttle back in neutral. Keep the steering wheel hard to starboard and apply a brief bump of reverse. This will slow or stop your forward momentum while helping to swing your boat's stern to the dock. You may need to apply a couple of these very brief bursts. When the boat is parallel to the dock, deploy dock lines and secure the vessel.

Again, the docking maneuver is easier for twin-engine boats, even though they're generally much larger and require more physical space to turn. Approach the dock at a 30- to 40-degree angle, with the steering wheel centered, gear in neutral and the throttles in their lowest idle position. As in the previous maneuvers, you will not use the steering wheel at all. Bump the drives simultaneously forward to keep the slowest possible momentum toward the dock. Just before the bow reaches the dock, bump the drives in reverse to stop the boat's movement. Now, again assuming a port-side docking, simultaneously bump the port drive forward and the starboard drive reverse. This will cause the boat to pivot. Don't work the throttles at all—just bump the drives into gear and back into neutral as needed to rotate the boat into position against the dock. Deploy dock lines and secure the boat.

Undocking in calm conditions is generally an easily accomplished maneuver, especially if you're undocking from a slip. In that situation, there's really only one key to success: Make sure you're completely clear of the slip and the boats in slips on the other side before starting a turn so you don't knock the bow or stern against them.

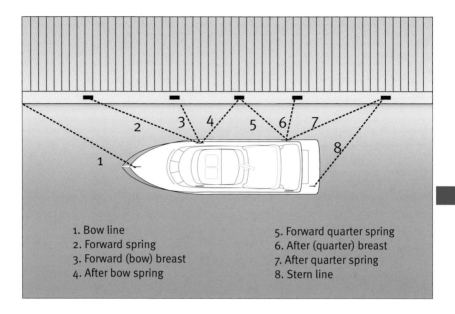

1. Bow line	5. Forward quarter spring
2. Forward spring	6. After (quarter) breast
3. Forward (bow) breast	7. After quarter spring
4. After bow spring	8. Stern line

All eight possible dock lines are shown here, but small crafts will never need to use them all at the same time.

Undocking from a parallel position, in calm conditions, is usually easiest to accomplish by having a dockhand give your boat a good shove and simply waiting until you've floated clear to pull away. Again, the most important thing to remember is to be patient and wait until the boat is well clear (at least a full boat length) of the dock before initiating a turn.

Docking into a Headwind or Current

It's common sense but worth repeating that if the wind and current are from the same direction, their effects will be magnified; if the wind and current are from opposite directions, their effects will be more or less cancelled out; and if the wind and current are from different directions, their effects will be altered according to which is stronger. The kind of boat you are in can make a lot of difference. Sailboats with big keels and their sails down will be more affected by current than wind, and powerboats with high profiles and relatively flat, shallow hulls will be affected more by wind than current.

For the purposes of this discussion, in a parallel docking situation, we'll define a headwind or current as a force running parallel with the dock. That said, let's start with a single-engine vessel.

If you're very lucky, the wind will be blowing or the current moving (and from here on, we're just going to say "wind;" understand that "current" also applies) so that you'll be able to head into it and still perform a port-side docking. If you're a little less lucky, you'll be facing the wind as you dock starboard-side.

The first key to docking into a headwind with an outboard or stern drive boat is to realize that by using steady power, you can essentially negate many of the wind's effects and hold a steady position. So you'll use essentially the same technique as in calm conditions, only with different amounts of throttle applied. Again, a shallower approach angle is best, as the wind will magnify any angle you take toward the dock: for example, if you're heading into the wind and turn slightly to port, the wind will catch the bow and push you harder in that direction. So you want to take a shallow approach angle and offer as little broadside to the wind as possible.

As you begin to plan your approach to the dock, deploy fenders and prepare dock lines well in advance. If possible, have dockhands or deck crew ready to assist. You should have a dock line already affixed to your bow cleat—this will be the spring line that's critical to the docking. (Some skippers set a spring from a midships cleat.)

Pick a target spot where you'll try to bring the bow to the dock and aim for that. You'll have to use a little extra throttle to overcome the wind, so instead of bumping the drive into forward and back to neutral, leave the drive engaged while using just enough power to move forward gently. Turn the wheel slightly to port to initiate the maneuver to the dock. The combination of momentum and wind will magnify the bow's pivot, so be gentle with the steering input. As soon as possible, pass the bow dock line ashore and make sure that it is secure it to the dock. Once the spring line is secured to both boat and dock, turn the steering wheel hard to port and put the drive in reverse. This will pull the stern to the dock, where you can deploy lines and secure the boat.

Docking is similar when running a single-engine inboard boat with right-hand prop. As you approach the dock in neutral at a shallow angle, turn the wheel to starboard and shift the gear to reverse. A quick thrust of the throttle will stop the forward movement and send the stern to the dock.

Twin-engine craft should approach a dock in a headwind at an angle. A line should be tied at the bow, and you should have someone ready to secure this line to the dock for use as a spring line at the earliest opportunity. Pull the boat alongside your intended docking position, then, leaving the steering wheel centered and both drives engaged in forward, use the throttles to hold the position into the wind. Assuming a port-side docking, gently and gradually increase starboard throttle. This will start the bow toward the dock. You may need to add a little port throttle to keep the boat in position or even moving ever so slightly forward. As soon as possible, toss the bow line ashore and secure it to the dock. Bring both throttles back to idle, then shift the starboard drive to reverse. This will swing the stern to the dock, at which time you can deploy lines and secure the boat.

Undocking from a parallel position into a headwind requires some planning. If the area behind your boat is clear, the best method is to get a good shove away from the dock with the wind moving the bow out. Let the boat drift well clear, then simply pull away. If there is a boat or obstacle behind you that prevents this method, use a bow line as a spring line. In a single-engine boat docked portside, turn the wheel hard to port and bump the throttle into forward. The bowline will pull the bow tightly against the dock (that's why it's important to have fenders deployed) while the stern swings wide to starboard. Once the stern is well clear of the obstruction (wait until the boat is nearly perpendicular to the dock), quickly center the wheel, release the spring line, and apply gentle reverse throttle until you're well clear of the dock. Now turn the wheel about halfway to starboard and bump the throttle into forward. You want to initiate a gentle turn, not a hard pivot, before pulling away safely.

In a twin-engine boat, use the same spring line, only instead of turning the wheel hard to port, leave the port drive in neutral and put the starboard drive in forward with both throttles in idle. As in the previous example, the boat will use the spring line as a fulcrum and the stern will swing out clear of the obstacle. Once clear, shift both drives to reverse, release the spring line, and apply gentle, simultaneous throttle to back away from the dock. When well clear, shift the starboard drive to neutral and the port drive to forward to straighten the boat so you can safely exit.

Winds from Other Directions

Docking in a following wind, which blows from your back, parallel to the dock, is a situation that can almost always be avoided: Simply turn around to approach the dock facing upwind. If turning around is impossible, proceed as above but secure the stern line first.

A wind that carries you toward the dock is generally a favorable condition, although it requires you to think and act a bit more quickly than in calm conditions, because the wind will make everything happen more rapidly. The general theory behind docking with a wind blowing you toward the dock is to get the boat into position early, then simply let the wind handle the rest. Usually, however, you'll need to do a little maneuvering, especially if you're trying to fit into a tight space.

The key to success is to leave lots of clear space between boat and dock. The larger your boat, the more the wind will affect it and the quicker that space will be used, so start with more distance than you think you'll need. For a portside docking in a single-engine outboard or stern drive boat, approach the dock, "aiming" the bow at a point just a bit left of the center point of your intended space. Approach at no more than idle speed. While you're still well away from the dock, apply a quick burst of reverse throttle with the steering wheel in the neutral position to slow your progress toward the dock, coming as near to a complete stop in the water as possible. Now, put the gear in neutral, turn the wheel hard to starboard, and then apply a quick burst of forward gear/throttle. This will start the boat's pivot but will also accelerate your momentum toward the dock, so your next move has to be done quickly. Shift the gear/throttle back to neutral, turn the wheel hard to port, then apply a sharp burst of reverse. This will swing the stern toward the dock.

At this point, you should be more or less parallel with the dock, turned fully broadside to the wind and drifting into your intended space. Center the steering wheel and bump the gear/throttle into forward or reverse as necessary to avoid bumping other boats or obstacles as you drift into the dock.

A twin-engine craft has an easier time with this type of docking. Approach the dock at a 30-degree angle. Approach at no more than idle speed. Well away from the

▓ Famous Flubs ▤

It's easy to underestimate how a wind that blows into the dock will affect your boat while docking, even if you're an experienced boater. Just ask Bo Elder.

"I'd been out wakeboarding with some friends," he remembers. "It was pretty calm when we started that morning, but by noon or so, it had gotten pretty breezy. We were hungry anyway, so we called it a day and were heading back to the launch ramp when I saw that we were just about out of gas. I didn't want to run out before we got back to the car, so I headed for the first gas dock I saw.

"This was one of those gas docks way out on the end of a pier, with a bunch of old tires tied in a big circle to act as a breaker, so the water's fairly calm around the dock, but there's nothing to break the wind at all. There was a little convenience store attached, so there were a couple of other boats tied up at the dock, with a space available right in front of the gas pump. That was all I needed, so that's where I went.

dock, apply simultaneous reverse throttle to slow your progress to as close to a halt as possible. Then, in rapid succession, without using the steering wheel at all and leaving the throttles in idle, leave the starboard drive in reverse and shift the port drive to forward. This will start the boat's pivot. You may need to apply a little added portside throttle to overcome the wind's pressure against your bow.

As soon as the boat is more or less parallel with the dock,

"As I'm pulling toward the dock, a guy comes out to pump the gas and he's standing there with a line in his hand, waiting for us. I've been driving ski boats most of my life, so I don't even give it a second thought when it comes to docking. I'll just slide us right in. But the wind's stronger than I think, and all of a sudden I realize that I'm coming in way too fast. The guy at the pump realizes it, too, and starts yelling, 'Back it off! Back it off!' Of course, at this point, I'm about 15 feet away from the dock and it's too late. I jam it into reverse but all that does is slow the boat down enough that when we smash into the dock I only knock a chunk out of the gel coat instead of bashing a big hole in the hull.

"Of course, the guy at the pump's yelling at me for hitting the dock so hard, my friends are yelling at me for banging them all around, and I'm yelling at myself for doing something so stupid and damaging my boat. The only good thing about the whole deal was that I didn't do any real damage to the dock, and I didn't hit any other boats.

"I just got a little overconfident and paid the price. About $250 for gel coat repair."

shift both drives to neutral and let the wind push you to the dock. You may need to bump the drives (simultaneously) into forward or reverse to fine-tune your approach, so don't get lazy at the helm.

Undocking with a wind that's blowing you back into the dock may seem like a daunting task, but it's really not that difficult. Use the same techniques as described previously for undocking into a headwind, with a bow spring line acting as a fulcrum to help you swing the stern away from the dock until the boat is almost perpendicular to the dock. At that point, cast off the spring line and apply steady reverse throttle to back the boat away from the dock quickly. When you're well clear of the dock, pivot the boat to starboard and exit safely.

Wind off the Dock

An "off the dock" wind is the most difficult docking condition most recreational boaters will ever face. Inevitably, the wind is strongest and the space into which you'll have to fit the boat is smallest when the crowd watching is the largest. This means you have two options: stay at sea until the wind calms, or perform an unpanicked, deliberate, most excellent docking that will win the admiration and respect of all who witness it. The choice is yours.

The problem in this scenario is that the wind is not only blowing you away from the dock but magnifying any maneuvers you make as you near the dock. Throttle mastery and good planning are the keys to overcoming the wind.

In a single-engine boat, approach the dock head-on, at a 90-degree angle, aiming the bow at a point approximately where the stern will contact the dock. A light but steady forward throttle will be required to overcome the wind and provide momentum toward the dock. In our experience, it's best to come to almost a complete stop in the water when the bow is a few feet from the dock. Put the gear/throttle in neutral long enough to turn the wheel hard to starboard (again, we're performing a port-side docking), then give a small bump of forward. This will initiate a right-hand turn. As the bow turns, the wind will catch it and exaggerate the steering input, so be gentle.

Now apply small bumps of forward, "working" the wind, so that you're essentially propelling the boat forward into the dock, while the wind is turning the bow away from the dock and settling you right into your intended space. A spring line can be very helpful here as well.

With a twin-engine boat, docking with a wind blowing you away from the dock is less difficult than docking in a single-engine craft, but it still requires some thought and effort. Approach the dock head-on, at a 90-degree angle, aiming the bow at the center point of your intended space. Bring the bow within a few feet of the dock, then use simultaneous reverse gears and throttles to stop your momentum. For a port-side docking, quickly shift the throttles to idle, the starboard drive to reverse, and the port drive to forward. The boat will pivot quickly, and as it does, add a little extra forward throttle to the port engine to counter the wind and keep the bow as close to the dock as possible.

As soon as possible, deploy dock lines and use them to pull the boat into the space. Once there, secure the boat.

Undocking with a wind blowing away from the dock is perhaps the easiest close-quarters maneuver there is. Simply cast off the lines and let the wind push you away from the dock until you're well clear of all obstacles, at which time you can safely exit the area.

Tying the Knot

You haven't docked until the boat is well and safely secured, and tying a compound version of a granny knot and hoping it holds doesn't count. Although there are hundreds, if not thousands, of knots and variations, there are really only six knots that an accomplished recreational boat handler should know: *bowline, anchor bend, sheepshank, cleat hitch, clove hitch,* and the *round turn & two half-hitches.*

BOWLINE The bowline is often called the "king of knots," because it's the single most useful knot in any boater's repertoire. A bowline is used to create a secure loop in a line that can then be slipped over a piling or a cleat. A properly tied bowline will not slip and is quickly and easily untied. If you only learn one knot, it should be the bowline.

ANCHOR BEND The anchor bend is used to affix the end of a line to a loop, such as you would find on an anchor or a mooring buoy. Sometimes called the fishermen's bend, it's also useful on fishing hooks and even water toys such as inflatables.

SHEEPSHANK A sheepshank is generally used to add strength to a worn section of line. It relieves the stress on the section, but also shortens the line. Make sure the worn area is centered within the knot, and replace the line at the earliest opportunity.

CLEAT HITCH The cleat hitch is the knot most frequently used to secure your boat to a dock. With a little practice, you'll be able to throw a cleat hitch as if you were a cowboy throwing a lasso.

CLOVE HITCH Use a clove hitch to secure your boat to a piling when the piling is too tall to allow you to lasso it with a bow line. A clove hitch is not a particularly secure knot and can easily come loose, so use it only if you're tying up temporarily.

ROUND TURN & TWO HALF HITCHES This is an extremely secure knot that can be used to permanently secure the boat to a piling or mooring buoy. It can also be used on an anchor or water toy.

CHAPTER 6

ANCHORING

I f there is one skill that is paramount in keeping you and your boat safe, it's anchoring. If your steering skills are rusty, you can correct them as you go, even if the wake is a little wiggly. But if your anchoring technique is bad, it could result in the boat coming adrift—which could mean serious trouble. You could be asleep, sunbathing, or reading a book and you might not notice the boat slowly drifting away until it hits the rocks.

Early anchors weren't much more than a big rock and a length of rope. Today we have efficient yet lightweight anchors that perform amazingly well. Still, the best anchor won't work right if you don't use it right.

The anchor you use and how you use it both depend on what you need it to do. If you are only going to anchor long enough to see if there are bass lurking around, your needs are different than if you are going to spend the night anchored in 30 feet of water.

Anchors work by digging into the bottom. For that to happen, the angle of pull has to be as close to parallel with the bottom as possible. This is accomplished by letting out more anchor line, called "rode," than the depth of the water. If you were in 10 feet of water and let out 10 feet of rode, the anchor would just touch the bottom and there would be no grab at all. Let out 20 feet and the anchor will still be nearly upright. But let out 70 feet, and the anchor will come at a low angle to the bottom and will dig in.

The amount of extra rode you let out is called scope, and it's expressed as a ratio: With the 70 feet of rode in 10 feet of water the scope is 7:1. Generally, a scope of 3:1 is the minimum amount that will work. But if you're going to stay for longer than a lunch break, consider 5:1 the minimum and 7:1 good for most anchorages.

To make your life easier, the rode should be marked at least every 10 feet. You can use paint to mark chain every 10 feet or so (at 30 feet, for example, you would paint three links) and if you're using rope, you can buy short strips of flexible plastic with numbers printed on them. Open up the strands and thread the plastic strips in between them. This system works very well because you can also feel the markers in the dark.

The anchor rode can be made of chain, rope, or a combination of the two. A rope rode is light and easy to stow, but if can fray if it rubs against rocks or coral. For this reason most skippers attach a short length of chain directly to their anchor, and use nylon rope for the rode. A length of chain equal to the length of the boat seems to work well.

An all-chain rode will hold on less scope than an all-rope rode, but you still shouldn't trust anything much less than 5:1 for anchoring overnight. Nylon rode has a lot of stretch, making the ride gentler, especially if the boat tugs up against the anchor because of the wind. Chain can bring the boat up in an abrupt manner, putting a lot of stress on the boat and the anchor. Smart sailors who have all-chain anchor rodes use a "snubber," a length of nylon rope with one end tied to the anchor chain and the other tied to a secure cleat on the boat. Let out enough chain so that it hangs below the nylon. The stretch in the nylon will be appreciated by your guests.

When you enter the anchorage, don't be in a hurry to get the hook down. Take a short tour of the area, watching the depth sounder and checking out how any other boats are lying. Brief your crew on what you're doing and what they will need to do. While you can drive the boat and put out the anchor by yourself, the process is a lot easier if you have someone on the bow taking care of the anchor while you coordinate the boat's position and set the anchor.

When you select a spot, check the depth and remember to add on the distance from the water to the anchor roller and to note the state of the tide. A 5:1 scope at low tide could easily become 3:1 at high tide. Add a little wind and your anchor may start to drag.

While sufficient scope is important, don't let out so much rode that your boat will swing around and hit other boats. More than one boat has been blown ashore or into a dock when the wind shifted, not because the anchor dragged, but because the boat moved around the firmly set anchor.

When you decide on the place to anchor, head to your spot while motoring into the wind. When the boat comes to a stop at the right place, note the depth and signal the bow crew to lower the anchor. Don't heave it off the side in a tangle of chain and rope. Lower it as quickly as possible until the anchor touches the bottom. If you've marked the rode every 10 feet or so you will know how much rode is out.

Let the wind blow you slowly back, away from the anchor, which is now sitting on the bottom. You might have to give things a hand with a bit of reverse. Try to pay out the rode at the same speed as the boat. You don't want the

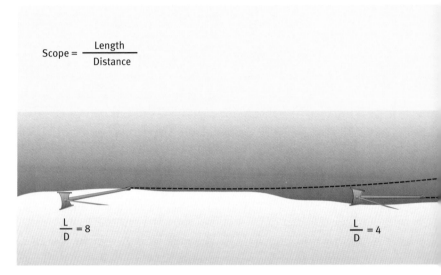

$$\text{Scope} = \frac{\text{Length}}{\text{Distance}}$$

$$\frac{L}{D} = 8 \qquad\qquad \frac{L}{D} = 4$$

Scope, the ratio of rode length L to the distance D, from the bow to the bottom (1), is critically important to safe anchoring. At (2) the rode length is twice the distance D, but the angle of pull tends to pull the anchor free. At (4), with L four

anchor rode to pile up on the bottom or tangle in the anchor, and you don't want to drag the anchor along the bottom.

When you've let out the calculated amount, have the crew secure the anchor rode. The windlass is not designed to take the strain of the anchor holding the boat in a breeze. Secure the rode, whether chain or rope, to a proper cleat or a chainstopper, a metal locking device that folds down between the links of chain.

The next step is to back up under power, slowly at first, to "set" the anchor. If you charge madly backwards it will just slide across the bottom. You will know when it sets hard. When the anchor is dragging, the bow crew can usually feel it by touching the rode. The rode will vibrate or jerk as the anchor bumps along. When the boat comes to a

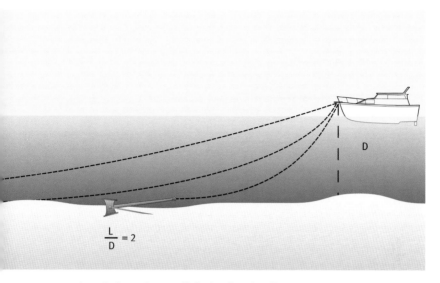

$\dfrac{L}{D} = 2$

times D, the anchor can dig in, but there is still too much upward pull on the rode. At (8) scope 8:1, the short length of chain at the anchor lies flat on the bottom, and any pull acts to pull the anchor in deeper.

stop, back off the throttle and shift into neutral. The boat will slowly move forward and come to a stop.

Take a look around to see where you are. If you have a hand-bearing compass, take a few bearings of objects on land. Write them down and compare the readings later to see if you're dragging. Set your GPS to the "anchor watch" mode. It will sound an alarm if that boat moves. Don't use the position of other boats to mark your position because they could drag.

If the anchor doesn't set, you will need to raise it up enough to be sure it hasn't picked up something. I have seen anchors drag up everything from washing machines to coils of cable to old lobster traps. Sometimes the anchor will roll up a ball of weeds and mud, but whatever you find on it, you will have to remove it and try again.

Try letting out more rode than you need, even 10:1 or 12:1. You may find that setting the anchor with the rode nearly parallel to the bottom will do the trick. Once the anchor is properly set, you can take up the rode so you don't swing into other boats.

Anchorage etiquette requires the latest boat in to drop anchor in a manner and place that doesn't interfere with other boats. Remember that other boats will swing on their anchors, but not necessarily in the same way as yours. Boats with all-chain rodes won't swing as far as those with rope rodes. Sailboats with deep keels will be more affected by current or tide. Boats with lots of freeboard and maybe a tuna tower will be more affected by wind.

Choosing the right anchor for the bottom condition is important, too. Your chart will tell you what the bottom is made of. Many skippers cruise with just one anchor, but if you have two, each one optimized for a different type of bottom, you'll sleep much better overnight in that perfect cove.

The final step is to let other boats know that you're at anchor. At night turn on the anchor light, called a white 360, a constant white light that is visible from anywhere around the boat. During the day, you use an anchor ball, a black ball shape you hang or place as high as possible. Most skippers use anchor balls made of two circles of black plastic that open up at right angles to each other. It looks like a ball but is about the size a large dinner plate when folded flat.

It may seem like overkill, and there are probably more recreational skippers who don't use anchor signals than ones who do, but consider the possible consequences if a boat hits you while you are at anchor. When the Coast Guard sets about assessing blame for the collision, the first question they will ask you will concern your anchor signals.

If you weren't displaying them, the Coast Guard generally won't have to look much further in their search for the cause.

If you are at all worried about the safety of your boat, perhaps because the wind is rising or there are other boats around that might bump into you if their anchors drag, remember that it's okay to get up a few times during the night to have a look around.

At the risk of over-simplification, anchors for recreational boats can be divided

A Delta is a one-piece plow anchor that holds well on a rocky bottom.

into three categories. There are plow anchors, such as the CQR, Delta, and Spade. Made of steel, they look like plows with a weighted point that digs into the bottom. You will see CQR or other plow anchors on the bows of many offshore boats because they are simple, strong, and made according to a design proven by years of use. Some, like the CQR, have a hinged plow section that allows the boat to move in relation to the anchor without the need for the anchor to reset itself. Others, like the Delta, are welded or forged into one piece. Plows do a good job of penetrating through grass and weeds and will catch on rocky bot-

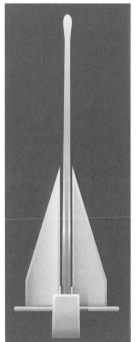

A Danforth is an example of a fluke anchor, good for sand or mud.

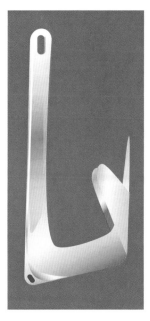

The Bruce anchor works well in sand and mud and is also strong enough for use in rocks.

toms. They typically need to be somewhat heavier than other anchors for a given boat size.

Plows are not ideal for sand or mud, which is where you would use fluke anchors, also called "Danforth" or "Danforth-style." These anchors deliver very high holding power for their weight, since the flukes are fairly large. Fluke anchors are made of steel or aluminum and, because they are nearly flat, stow easily on deck. The Fortress aluminum fluke anchors disassemble easily and can be stowed anywhere.

The third category is the "claw" anchor. Nearly all of them resemble the original claw, the Bruce anchor, which was designed to hold offshore oilrigs in the North Sea. Claw anchors set easily, are very strong, and have no moving parts, but they are bulky and difficult to stow on a bow roller. Like the CQR, Bruce anchors are often seen on the bows of offshore boats.

There are other types of anchors, like mushroom anchors and grapnels, but these are more suitable for dinghies and small, open boats. So-called "stockless" or "navy-type" anchors do not deliver powerful holding relative to their weight. They are designed to self-launch and stow easily on large boats that can carry an anchor that might weigh several tons. The traditional "fisherman's anchor" looks just like a cartoon anchor, and these are still in use by some sailors. However, despite their usefulness for rocky bottoms, they have to be very heavy to hold. Stick with plow, fluke, or claw anchors.

Anchor manufacturers have charts telling you which anchor they recommend based on a boat's length. Don't cheat and use the next smaller size; follow the recommendations. The anchor is the only thing that stands between your boat and a collision.

Most of the time a single anchor, properly placed and set well, is enough to hold your boat. There are occasions, though, when another anchor is necessary. There may be a storm coming or you may be in a crowded anchorage and need to reduce your swinging room. You may be anchored in a channel where the tidal current is strong and reverses with every cycle.

The most common method of setting two anchors is to place them at an angle of between 30 and 60 degrees from each other. Set the first anchor and then motor over, perpendicular to the wind, to where you will place the second anchor. Let the boat fall back, driven by the wind, as you pay out rode in the usual manner. Set the anchors just as though you were using a single anchor. Since you have two anchors out, you will be able to get by with less scope, an advantage in crowded or small anchorages.

You can also use your dinghy to set the second anchor, after you are sitting to a properly set first anchor. Put the anchor in the dinghy and with your crew feeding anchor rode to you, take the dinghy out and put the anchor over the side. The crew can then take in rode and set the anchor.

If you're in a narrow anchorage, you can set two anchors so that you are in the middle between them, called a Bahamian moor. While you may go years without actually needing a Bahamian moor, if you do need it, nothing else

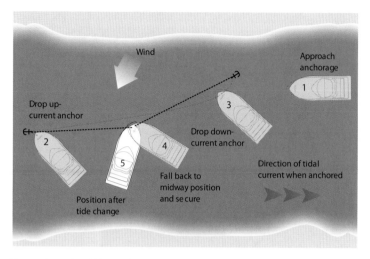

Two anchors should be set from the bow in a "Bahamian moor" when anchoring in a narrow waterway with reversing tidal current.

will hold you in place as well. Set the first anchor and motor out twice the distance you plant to let out the rode. Put the second anchor over and then, taking in the first rode, slowly maneuver the boat so you are equidistant between the two anchors.

Weighing Anchor

It's Sunday morning, you've just finished a perfect breakfast in the cockpit and it's time to weigh anchor and head back home. Last night the wind picked up a bit and your anchor held perfectly, but with the boat pulling on it for several hours, the anchor is probably buried deeply into the mud.

The first thing to do is go over the procedures with your

crew. To bring the anchor up it is almost imperative that you have someone in the bow. This person will direct you so the boat ends up directly above the anchor without putting strain on the windlass. It's important to remember that the windlass is not designed to move the boat. It is made to raise and lower the anchor rode, and if you use it to drag the boat up to the anchor, you will wear it out years before its time.

Your bow crew will gesture with arm motions in the direction of the rode so you can slowly drive the boat in that direction. As you move the boat, the crew will operate the windlass and take up the rode.

When you brief the crew, emphasize that the windlass can be a dangerous machine. Never touch the chain or the rode as it is being taken in. If the chain jams, stop the windlass and let the boat move up on the anchor so the strain is off the rode before you do anything. When the rode is straight down and you are above the anchor, the crew will secure the rode, either with a chainstopper or a cleat.

At that point, slowly motor past where the anchor is located, in the opposite direction from the position the boat had relative to the anchor. If the boat spent the night directly south of the anchor, for example, you would motor north until you were over the anchor. The crew would then tie off the anchor rode while you very slowly continue north.

When the movement of the boat trips the anchor, you will probably feel it release. When it does, try putting the transmission in neutral until the anchor is nearly out of the water. Keep an eye on the rode as it comes up, especially the chain that had been lying on the bottom. Your crew should rinse mud and dirt off the chain and anchor with a deck-washing pump and hose or a long-handled scrub brush. If there is a lot of mud on the anchor you might find it helpful to leave the anchor in the water as you slowly motor, letting the water loosen the mud.

If the anchor doesn't release easily, take up the rode until the boat is directly over the anchor. Using some light line (yet another use for that big hank of quarter-inch line you bought at the army surplus store), tie a small loop in one end around the rode and ballast it with some fishing weights. If you have a short piece of plastic tubing, thread the loop through it to keep the loop open.

Get in your dinghy, lower the line down to the bottom, and then slowly motor out away from the boat. Keep the line slack so that it doesn't ride up the rode and when you are at 5:1 (or more) scope, give it a good pull. Tie it to the dinghy's bow and reverse away from it. The idea is that the loop will sink to the anchor and slide down the shank far enough so that you are now pulling the anchor out from the obstruction.

Still no luck? Time to call a diver. If you have to leave, cut the rode and attach a float to mark the spot. If you're worried that the float might attract someone who wants to salvage your anchor for himself, cut the rode so that the float is a few feet below the surface. Take a GPS reading and give it to the diver you hire.

If the anchor won't budge, even if you do everything right, you'll wish you had set the anchor with a trip line. If you're anchoring in a place where the ground is known to be foul or if you just worry about losing that expensive anchor, a trip line can be a good thing.

Take a look at your anchor down near the bottom, where the shank meets the flukes. You will see a small hole or, on CQR-type anchors, a U-shaped "handle" half an inch long or so. Tie a length of small line (quarter-inch three-strand polyester filament is perfect, with a breaking strength of 2,000 pounds.) through the hole and attach a float to the other end. Since you want it to float above the anchor, the line only needs to be slightly longer than the water depth. Coil up the extra line and hang it below the float. You'll need it later when you use the trip line. If you don't have a float, a docking fender works perfectly.

To trip the anchor, take the trip line on board and motor in the opposite direction from the way the anchor was set. Let out anchor rode as you go so that you don't create any strain on the anchor. When you are at about 3:1 scope with the trip line and the anchor rode is slack, tie the trip line to a cleat and slowly pull in the opposite direction from the way you were anchored. For example, if your boat spent the night lying south of the anchor, pull on the trip line with your boat north of the anchor.

The trip line should pull the anchor out from under whatever it was stuck on, which could be anything from a rock ledge to an uncharted wreck.

CHAPTER 7

MANEUVERING

The only way to know how your boat handles in any given set of circumstances is to have handled that particular boat in those circumstances. This should be all the justification anyone needs to get out on the water and spend time onboard. In other words, practice. Novices and old salts alike should follow a few common-sense guidelines when practicing boat handling.

- Always practice in the most open, least-busy waters available. When you're practicing, you're often maneuvering erratically, changing speeds and course suddenly. The captains of other boats won't be ready for it if you come to an abrupt stop or suddenly accelerate into a hard turn.

- Be aware of your surroundings. Maintain a constant, 360-degree lookout and don't attempt any maneuvers until you've made sure you won't be encountering any other boats, docks, or channel markers, and that there is no risk of running aground.

- Don't push the envelope. It's hard to imagine a justifiable reason for throwing your boat into a wheel-lock turn at full throttle. The goal is to learn how to control your boat—not to learn at what point you lose control of your boat.

Slow-Speed Maneuvering

Whether you're making your way through a maze of slips at a marina or waiting your turn at a gas dock, if you're a recreational boater, you will spend a lot of time operating at or near idle speed. Generally speaking, the slower the speed, the easier it is to handle your boat, simply because you have more time to take action. It is also important to master your maneuvers carefully, because even at slow speeds, a boat is pushed through the water by a propeller. And propeller rotation has, arguably, the most obvious affect on how a boat will handle at slow speeds, at least on single-engine boats. (Twin-engine boats are usually set up so that the two propellers rotate in opposite directions, thereby canceling out any rotational effects.)

To simplify dramatically, a propeller has angled blades that push the boat through the water. As these blades rotate, they encounter resistance—more as they go deeper, less as they spin toward the surface. Because of this torque action, the stern of the boat will tend to push in the opposite direction of the propeller's rotation.

For example, if a propeller rotates clockwise, at slow speeds you would expect the stern to move to starboard at first because of torque and then slightly to port due to prop wash. And since a boat will always tend to pivot on its center point, if the stern is pushed to port, the bow will head to starboard. This is why, since the vast majority of marine drive units are designed so that the propeller rotates clockwise, virtually every recreational boat will make a slow, gentle, right-hand turn if the drive is put in idle-forward and hands are off the steering wheel.

Because of propeller rotation effects, most boats will have a significantly smaller turning radius (at slow speeds) in one direction (usually to starboard). And as mentioned in Chapter 5, propeller rotation effects can make a single-engine boat, under reverse throttle, seem to go almost straight to one side (usually port) rather than backwards. Clearly, there are situations where either of these minor side effects can be beneficial, provided you know about them and are therefore able to use them to your advantage.

Propeller rotation can work against you, however, by expanding your boat's expected turning radius, by not reversing as anticipated, and even by initiating a turn without any input from you at the helm. So it's important that you know exactly to what extent your boat is affected by propeller rotation at slow speeds.

Bear in mind that hull size and design play roles in how much your boat is affected by propeller rotation. A sailboat with a keel will be much less affected by the propeller rotation of its outboard engine than a small, flat-bottomed, tournament ski boat. Most recreational boats are also affected by what's commonly known as "bow steer," which can interact with prop rotation. Bow steer results when the entry point of the hull is pushed to one side or the other by current or wave action, or, more often, by the turn initiation of the propeller rotation. As the bow's entry point slices into the water, if there's more pressure to one side or the other, the bow will be pushed in the opposite direction.

That's pretty simple. But once the bow begins to turn, the hull presents even more surface area to the high-pressure side and the turn is accelerated. At that point, the captain usually notices the bow wandering to one side and tries to correct it by steering in the opposite direction. This not only reverses the process but magnifies it, and the next thing you know the captain is working the wheel back and forth, carving a wavy line through the marina like a drunken sailor wandering home after a late night at the pub.

The best way to deal with both propeller rotation effects and bow steer is to reduce your input from the helm to the bare minimum necessary to keep the boat moving and under control. When it comes to boat handling, especially in slow speeds, remember that "Less Is More." Other than bolting on a keel, there's really not a lot you can do about your boat's susceptibility to bow steer or propeller rotation other than learn how it behaves and gently correct that behavior when it presents itself. To overcome the instinct to overcorrect, focus beyond your bow.

Pick a point well off the bow—on the horizon if you're in open water, or the point where you'll be making your next turn if you're in tighter quarters—and only make steering adjustments as needed to maintain a steady course toward that point. You'll be amazed by how much less you work the steering wheel or tiller, and how much better your boat seems to handle.

Another key to slow-speed handling is to learn the art of station keeping, or staying in one spot even in wind or current. This is a valuable skill if you need to pick up a downed skier or assist in a rescue. It's also one of the very best ways to practice your slow-speed handling skills and learn your boat's characteristics.

Station keeping is sometimes likened to hovering in a helicopter, without having to worry about how far off the ground you are. Like the pilot, however, a captain has to pay attention to wind. You'll also need to be aware of wind's soulmate, current. There's only one way to deal with wind and current: align your boat so the bow is heading into it and then keep that alignment. (If you're dealing with wind and current from different directions, you have to figure out which is affecting you more strongly. Adjust your handling accordingly.)

To practice station keeping, find some open water with a light breeze or current (we'll say breeze from here on; remember that current applies as well), and turn the boat so the bow is heading directly into the breeze. To hold your position, apply at least intermittent bursts of forward throttle. You may well have to use constant, steady throttle. The key is to start with as little forward throttle as possible—just the briefest of bumps—and add power only as required to keep the boat from drifting backwards.

Now comes the tricky part. The wind will push your bow to one side or the other. Even if you're aligned perfectly into the wind, your propeller rotation will ensure that the bow will move enough to catch some wind. This will perfectly replicate bow steering in calm conditions, so you can practice overcoming it. The instant the bow begins to move to one side, counter by steering just a wee bit in the opposite direction. The earlier you countersteer, the less effect there will be to counter. Note how quickly the bow responds, and how easy it is to overcorrect so that the bow is now being pushed the other way.

As you work the steering wheel and the throttle, you'll develop a strong, almost intuitive feel for how your boat is responding to your input, and more important, for how your boat is about to respond to outside forces. Once you've mastered station keeping, dealing with the effects of bow steer and prop rotation in close quarters will be a breeze.

Maneuvering at Speed

Virtually all recreational powerboats have planing hulls, which handle and perform best when the boat is traveling at speed. Sailboats with keeled hulls and power yachts have hulls that are designed differently, but even these boats deliver more precise, predictable handling when they're traveling at speed. It's important to mention that in a powerboat with a planing hull, the boat's handling will suffer tremendously when the boat's speed is between idle and planing speed, a condition known as plowing. At this speed, the bow rides high in the air, possibly obstructing the captain's view, and the hull is being forced through the water at an attitude that practically eliminates its handling characteristics and creates a massive wake.

At this speed, turns are difficult to initiate. A brief period of plowing is, of course, unavoidable when accelerating from idle to planing speed, or when slowing, but you should never operate the boat at plowing speed for any length of time, for any reason. If the boat can't achieve planing speed. slow to idle and head for the first available port.

A powerboat will handle most precisely and predictably at planing speeds, which will differ from boat to boat. At speed, the hull's hydrodynamics not only counter any propeller rotation effects but also work to respond to any steering input. Some hulls will actually hold a remarkably straight and steady course at speed, but even these hulls will react to variables such as waves and wind, so the captain should maintain control of the throttle and steering wheel at all times. Many boats, however, for reasons ranging from hull design to rudder tuning, will tend to pull to one side or the other, just like a car that needs alignment.

Whether your boat tracks as straight as an arrow or pulls to one side, holding a steady course at speed is the most fundamental of boat handling skills.

The key to holding a steady course is, as explained above, to look beyond the bow. Pick a landmark on the horizon or opposite shore, and simply drive straight toward that point. Keep one hand on the steering wheel and the other on the throttle. Maintain a steady speed. Apply as little steering

A power boat handles most predictably and precisely on plane.

input as possible to maintain a straight path to your chosen landmark. If the bow wanders to port (for example), steer to starboard just enough to stop the wandering, but not so much as to turn the bow to starboard. If you simply stop the wandering, the hull will tend to straighten itself out due to hydrodynamic design and the intrinsic gyroscopic effect of traveling at speed. If you try to steer the boat back on course, you'll actually overcorrect and find you're weaving from port to starboard.

To check your success at carving a straight path, use your rear-view mirror or glance over your shoulder and look at your boat's wake. Any weaving will show up clearly in a snaky wake that means you need more practice at holding a steady course. A straight wake means you're practicing just enough: Keep it up.

Turning at speed is a simple matter of maintaining a steady speed while you gradually turn the steering wheel until the boat carves the arc you desire. Note the word "gradually" to describe how you should work the steering wheel when making a turn at speed. Your steering input should inversely mirror your boat's speed: The faster the boat is going, the less you should turn the wheel to initiate a turn. It's better to leave yourself room to increase your

▨ Famous Flubs ☰

Dan Flatley (not his real name), a former marine journalist, knows just how dangerous hooking can be.

"I was testing a Four Winns runabout," Flatley remembers. "This was in the mid-1990s. I was at the helm, a representative from Four Winns was in the passenger seat, and a colleague of mine who shall remain nameless was sitting behind me. The boat had Super-Sport seating, so my colleague was facing backwards.

"We're doing speed runs, checking the boat's top speed with a GPS unit, and the Four Winns rep tells me, 'This hull can handle 4Gs.' He says it very nonchalantly, so I think he's pulling my leg, and I say so. ' No,' he insists. 'We've tested it. This hull can handle a 4G turn.' I tell him I'm going to have to call his bluff. 'Go ahead,' he says. I tell him to hang on, I tell my colleague to hang on, and I get a grip on the wheel. We're running wide open, probably 45 miles per hour or so. 'Everybody ready?' I yell. They say they are, so I throw the boat into a full left-hand turn.

"At that point, everything happened very quickly. The boat hooked like a monster, essentially making a 90-degree turn at 45 miles an hour. I got thrown into input than to be in a position of trying to counteract a movement. You can always turn the wheel more sharply, but you can't always spin it the other way.

At planing speed, you'll usually want to carve gentle arcs rather than sharp corners. If you sharpen the turn, you'll find that as you turn the steering wheel harder, the boat

the windshield so hard that I put a dent in the windshield's frame and wound up with a lump the size of a golf ball on my forehead. The guy from Four Winns was more or less unscathed.

"The bad news was my colleague. He somehow wound up wedged into the very corner of the boat, at the transom, on the passenger side. He'd been thrown diagonally the length of the boat, and he was sitting there with a blank look on his very, very ashen face. I cut the engine and asked if he was okay. 'I don't think so,' he said. 'I can't really move my arm.' That's when I noticed that his left hand was flopped limply in his lap, and his arm was at kind of an odd angle. 'I think I need to get to a hospital,' he said.

"I got us back to the dock as quickly, smoothly, and safely as I could. We called 911 en route, so the ambulance arrived almost as soon as we did. As it turned out, my colleague suffered a broken shoulder and pretty heavy bruises to his ribs. He wasn't a young guy, either, something like 67 years old at the time, so he wasn't able to just shake it off. He was unable to work for about three months. He never held it against me, that I could tell, but every time I saw him, I felt awful about what happened. I was stupid and he paid the price."⚓

slows down, even with the throttle held steady. This happens because as the boat turns more sharply, more of the hull contacts the water, increasing friction and slowing the boat. To correct this, increase throttle as you feel the boat slowing during the turn. As you pull out of the turn and the hull returns to plane, you'll feel the boat accelerating. That's when it's time to pull back on the throttle a bit.

However, sometimes you'll need to make a fairly sharp, fairly sudden turn. If you're pulling a skier who goes down, you'll need to spin around and retrieve him or her as quickly as possible. In these situations, it's important to avoid simply turning the steering wheel as far as it will go without making some adjustments to your speed. The reason why has to do with how planing hulls are designed.

Planing hulls are not smooth. Look closely and you'll see ridges, called strakes. As the hull passes through the water, these strakes channel and direct the water, giving the hull its bite. This is especially important when turning. Without strakes, a planing hull would tend to slide, making for sloppy handling at best, dangerous handling at worst. The strakes enable the hull to grab the water and stop the slide, providing more precise, predictable handling.

The downside to this is that the strakes aren't adjustable. When they come into contact with the water, no matter how fast the boat is going, they grab and redirect the hull's path of travel. At higher speeds, this leads to the phenomenon known as hooking, where the hull grabs the water suddenly and violently changes the boat's direction. At moderate speeds, this effect is simply unpleasant. At high speeds, it's very dangerous, capable of throwing people and gear around and out of the boat.

If you have to make a sudden, sharp turn, start by backing off the throttle and slowing the boat. This will make the turn safer and actually make it easier for you to turn the steering wheel, especially in an inboard with a rudder. The rudder turns by pushing against the water, but the faster the boat is traveling, the more the pressure of the water tries to keep the rudder pointed in the direction of least resistance—that is, straight ahead.

Having slowed the boat slightly, turn the steering wheel. As soon as you feel that the boat has initiated the turn, start adding throttle. As you increase the throttle, turn the steering wheel more. This will power the boat into and through a very tight turn without risk of hooking the hull.

Traffic and Etiquette

If you're the only boat on the water, you can pretty much do anything you want that doesn't endanger you, your passengers, or your craft. Unfortunately, it's becoming more and more of a rarity to find yourself alone on the water. From Miami to Seattle, boating traffic is on the increase on just about every inch of navigable water. This means that developing good boat handling skills, more than ever, also involves learning the rules that govern marine traffic and etiquette.

The definitive book on marine traffic rules has already been written: the U.S. Coast Guard's *Navigation Rules*, which is available online for free at http://www.navcen. uscg.gov/mwv/navrules/navrules.htm. It also can be ordered from the U.S. Government Printing Office (Stock# 050-012-00407-2) for $15, so we won't replicate the guide's highly detailed information here. We will recommend that anyone planning to navigate heavily trafficked coastal waters or international waters should get a copy and study it diligently. It's a good idea for all boaters to learn the inland section.

CHAPTER 8

ENGINE TRIM AND TABS

The drive units on an outboard, or the outboard drive legs, can be adjusted throughout a range of motion that extends from having the propellers out of the water to having them tucked in close to the transom. That movement is known as engine trim, or more accurately, trimming the drive.

If you ask most boaters how engine trim affects their boats, they'll say it raises or lowers the bow. Some might mention that trimming can increase or decrease top speed, or that it can soften the ride in rough water, but you won't hear a lot of discussion of the major role engine trim can play in how a boat handles. It's time to correct this oversight. An improperly trimmed engine can severely compromise your boat's handling characteristics, as well as dramatically reduce your boat's overall performance. On the other hand, a properly trimmed engine will help your boat perform better and more economically, as well as deliver the best possible handling at speed.

Although engine trim is tremendously variable, we divide it into three main classifications: trim in (often called trim down), neutral trim, and trim out (often called trim up). For many boaters, especially novices, these can be somewhat confusing terms. Part of that reason may be because trim in and trim out refer to the drive leg position, whereas trim down and trim up refer to the result of that trim. If you trim in, the result of that movement is to force the bow down.

Neutral trim refers to the drive unit's propeller being perpendicular to the surface of the water. Moving the prop towards the transom changes the angle of the prop to the surface of the water, a process that forces the bow down. Move the prop out, and the direction of the prop's force pushes the transom down and the bow up. That's the simple explanation of how the engine is trimmed. Now let's find out why.

If you look at a boat with a planing hull while it's out of the water, you'll notice that the underside of the hull is not flat. There is a flatter section of hull aft near the transom, but as you go forward toward the bow the hull angles up to meet the point of the bow. This angle of entry achieves several effects. Its primary purpose is to act as a sort of lever to raise the bow when the boat is in motion, so the hull will come up on plane and ride on the small, flat running surface near the transom. You can clearly see this in action by accelerating a planing-hulled boat from idle while the engine is in neutral trim. As the boat accelerates, the bow will rise, allowing the boat to "come out of the hole." Once on plane, the bow will drop down, but will continue to ride at a slightly raised angle. The secondary purpose of this angle of entry is to help the bow slice through the water at slower speeds.

As you've probably guessed, engine trim is used to enhance, and in some cases overcome, the inherent properties of a well-designed planing hull. If the boat is wallowing in a no-wake zone, with the bow so high you can't see where you're going, trimming the drives all the way in may provide some relief. While there are variations in the amount of effect, each of the three main trim settings delivers certain specific results.

Trimming in (or trimming down) lowers the bow. This is most often used when accelerating from idle, as it helps overcome the bow's tendency to rise and will bring the boat up on plane more quickly, especially if there's a heavy load or a large number of passengers near the transom. At speed, trimming in and lowering the bow will deliver a smoother ride in choppy water, as the sharp edge of the bow is brought into play to slice through the rough water. Trimming in and lowering the bow does, however, increase the amount of hull surface in contact with the water, so it will reduce top speed and, in most boats, increase the amount of steering torque or pull to starboard. Too much trim down and the boat will begin to steer poorly.

Neutral trim is the default setting, neither enhancing nor reducing performance and handling.

Trimming out (trimming up) raises the bow. This reduces the amount of hull surface in contact with the water, so it will increase the boat's speed (even if you don't increase throttle). Trimming out also reduces the boat's draft, even at slow speeds, so it's often applied in shallow areas. Trimming out will tend to increase the boat's tendency to pull to port, but its greatest drawback is that if you trim out too much, the boat will tend to bounce—sometimes called "porpoising"—in the water, a jarring and unpleasant experience. Fortunately, trimming in and lowering the bow can almost always eliminate porpoising.

If you find the boat continues to porpoise, even fully trimmed in, it might be because you have too much weight in the bow. The prop doesn't have enough drive to raise the bow and the weight, so get those extra people out of the bow and move the coolers aft, perhaps to the cockpit.

Trimming up a stern drive is also a good strategy for shallow water and slow speeds. With the drive unit trimmed so that the prop is barely in the water, you can navigate water barely deep enough to float the boat. With the drive this far out, don't try for any speed records; all you will do is throw up a lot of water. This "rooster tail" is not

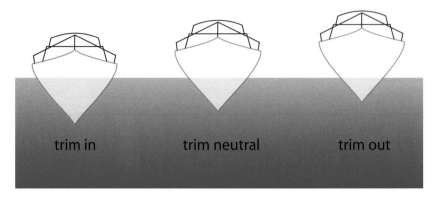

trim in   trim neutral   trim out

Trimming in lowers the bow. Trimming out raises it.

much more than wasted gas, although it does look impressive (until the spectators notice that you're only going 15 knots). Exceeding speeds much faster than a crawl with the drive trimmed all the way out will also push the stern down, making you draw more water, which is the wrong thing to do when the bottom is so close.

Trimming is easily accomplished on most stern drives via a rocker switch on the throttle control. Learning proper trim technique is a matter of practice because the only way to know when your boat is properly trimmed is by feel. A few basic exercises will get you familiar with the technique, and then you only have to practice.

Bring the boat up on plane with the engine in neutral trim and hold a steady throttle, then gently trim the engine all the way out and all the way in to see and feel how the trim affects the boat's attitude, ride, and handling. Don't adjust the throttle while you're doing this. As you experiment, you'll discover a sweet spot where the boat suddenly achieves peak performance; if you trim in or out even a little from this point, performance decreases noticeably.

Make a note of your speed and the trim gauge indicator. In the future, when you're traveling near this speed, you'll be able to use the trim gauge to trim the engine quickly to approximately the optimal position. Of course, due to variables such as wind, sea condition, and the number of people on board, you'll still have to rely on feel to find the perfect trim setting at any given moment. Over time, you'll develop an instinctive feel for trimming your boat at almost any speed, in almost any conditions. The important thing you will learn is how the boat feels when it needs trim up as opposed to when it needs trim down.

If you have an inboard engine with a standard rudder, you will only be able to adjust hull trim, using the two trim tabs visible on either side of the transom at the waterline.

Trim tabs are adjustable plates that when used in tandem, can achieve results similar to engine trim on powerboats that don't have trimmable drives. However, because they consist of two plates that can be adjusted independently, trim tabs are much more versatile and effective in terms of improving a boat's ride, handling, and performance in any water condition. (Even on twin-engine stern drive powerboats, trimming the engine results in adjusting the trim of both engines or drives simultaneously.)

If you look at a powerboat hull, from the rear when it's out of the water, you'll see that the "V" runs the length of the hull. In smaller runabouts, especially those intended for use in generally calm waters and on planing hulls, the "V" is dramatically reduced at the transom but still noticeable. In larger boats, and most boats that are intended for rough-water or offshore use, the "V" is sharper to provide a smoother ride. However, that sharper "V" means that at speed, the boat will have a tendency to lean to one side or the other, depending on such factors as wind, current, and even the position of people and gear on board. Trim tabs can be used to augment the effects of drive unit trim, or they can work independently to overcome the list that can result from wind, current, or load.

If you are battling big waves, the impact of those waves can be lessened if you trim the bow down. That is because the "V" of the bow will hit the waves first, splitting them and dissipating some of their energy. If those waves hit the flatter, aft portion of the hull, it will slam, loud and hard. Besides being uncomfortable, this action puts a lot of strain on the hull structure. If you trim too much in, you will start taking water over the bow because of the reduced freeboard and the boat will steer sluggishly and feel heavy. When you turn, the stern will slide out and the bow will dig in, a condition called "bow steering."

Trim Tabs in Action

As you accelerate from idle, you trim the drive units and the trim tabs all the way to "Bow Down" to lower the bow and come up on plane quickly. As the boat comes on plane, you trim to "Bow Up" until you find the sweet spot when the boat is cruising optimally. A strong wind begins blowing from port; the boat tries to list to starboard. To counter this effect, use the trim tab control to move the starboard-side tab toward "Bow Down." This has the effect of rolling the boat to port, and countering the list.

Of course, the deployed starboard-side trim tab is going to be subject to substantially more drag than the less-exposed portside tab. As a result, the boat will pull to port, so you'll have to increase your steering input accordingly. The deployed starboard-side tab will also slow the boat slightly, and you may need to adjust the drive trim and the trim tabs further to stay in the boat's performance sweet spot.

Because they function by deflecting water as the hull travels, trim tabs are more effective at higher speeds. At low speeds, the water travels around the tabs fairly easily and reduces the tabs' effect. As the hull travels faster, however, the relative density of the water increases and the tabs' effect becomes greater. As a result, it's usually recommended that you not use trim tabs when traveling slower than planing speed, because the tabs simply don't work that well at slow speeds. The exception to this rule of thumb is when, as mentioned above, you're accelerating from idle. In this case, shifting both trim tabs to full "Bow Down" setting will help the boat plane more quickly.

You can also use the trim tabs as a brake. Trimming in (or down) will drop the bow off a plane earlier than it would with the trim fully out, thus increasing drag. If you trim in, and cut the throttle, you will slow down rapidly. Be careful about shifting into reverse at high speeds. It can damage the gear set, and it isn't effective anyway because the prop will simply cavitate (review Chapter 3 for a full explanation of cativation).

You can also use the drag of a deployed trim tab to assist in steering, at least when traveling at speed. If you deploy the portside tab fully, for example, by moving the switch all the way to "Bow Down," the drag created by that tab will make it slightly easier to make a tight turn to port.

It's worth noting that engine trim and trim tabs are not mutually exclusive. In fact, they are both available on many boats, including some boats less than 20 feet in length. Used in concert, engine trim and trim tabs add tremendously to a captain's ability to keep the vessel performing optimally in all conditions, at all speeds.

CHAPTER 9

ONE ENGINE / TWO ENGINES

To be truly in charge of your boat, you need to understand how the engine and its propeller relate to your vessel's handling. This rule applies to whether your boat has one engine or two. The handling characteristics of a boat with one prop are very different from those of a boat with two props. A boat with a single prop has to cope with prop walk, as we explained in Chapter 3—that is, the tendency of the boat to turn, when moving forward, in the direction of the prop's rotation.

Boats with twin props are spared most of the problems with prop walk. Although some twin-prop boats that have both props rotating in the same direction, the standard now is to have the props rotate so that the tops of the propeller blades turn out. The starboard prop is a right-hand prop, and the port prop is a left-hand prop.

When maneuvering at slow speeds, nothing compares with the ease and agility of twin props. With the starboard prop going forward and the port prop in reverse, the boat will pivot practically in its own length, rotating in a counter-clockwise direction. When you put the port prop in forward and the starboard prop in reverse, you will rotate clockwise.

If you vary the relative throttle settings, you can alter the way the boat pivots. Give more power to the forward prop, and your pivot will become a very tight turn in the direction of the side that is in reverse. The rudders will give you some added control, but mostly on the side with the forward-turning prop, because of prop wash. In most maneuvers of this kind, you won't be going fast enough to cause a significant flow of water along the rudder that isn't being affected by the prop.

Give more power to the reverse prop and you will back down in a tight, controllable turn, with no need for rudder movement. There will still be a tendency for the rudders to kick over to the stops when in reverse, so keep a hand on the wheel while you are adjusting the throttles.

The ability to spin the boat in its own length is useful for more than making turns. If you are approaching your mooring and you find yourself with the mooring a few feet to the left of the bow, put the port prop in reverse, the starboard prop in forward, and the bow will, as if by magic, swing to the left and allow your crew to pick up the mooring.

The other part of maneuvering a twin that is different from maneuvering a single is backing down. With the two props rotating in opposite directions, there is no prop walk but you still need to keep your hand on the wheel. Now there are two rudders to catch in the water, and the same sort of problems can occur if you let them get out of control. When a rudder bangs against the stops, it can damage the rudder stops inside the boat or even the rudders themselves.

You can adjust the direction the boat backs down by varying the throttle settings or even shifting one engine into forward if you need to make tight turns. For gradual adjustments, such as backing into a slip, you will probably find that you can get your boat where you need it by using the throttle. The boat will turn in the direction opposite the side of the engine that you are giving more throttle.

When you pull away from the dock and are underway, there is another twin-related matter to deal with: The engines need to be synchronized. You accelerate with your twin engines just as with a single engine: Push the throttle forward until you are at the desired speed. Trim the boat and then listen to the engines. Chances are you will hear them throbbing, making a slow pulsing sound.

The engines need to be turning over at exactly the same speed. When they are off by as little 10 or 15 rpm, they can cause vibration and excessive noise, and this condition will also affect fuel economy, because the load isn't being equally shared between the engines. You may also find automatic engine synchronizers useful, especially if you operate the boat from the flybridge where you can't hear the engines well. You can synchronize your engines either by reading the indicator lights or the tachometers to tell you when the engines are exactly in synch. But there's no substitute for listening to the engines to get them in synch.

Most analog tachometers are not accurate enough for you to know the engines are in synch just by looking at the dials. Digital tachs are accurate to within a few rpm, and the indictor lights, which will blink in unison when the engines are together, are good as a reference. But once you've done it a few times, your ears will be tuned to tell you when you've got the engines running together.

If you find yourself constantly needing to fiddle with the throttle settings, possibly the throttle cables are loose or the springs aren't tensioned properly. It may be time to do some maintenance.

When you approach synchronizing the two engines, you will hear, and probably feel, a slow vibration that goes up and down, maybe a few seconds per cycle. Gradually move one of the throttles up. If the noise increases in frequency, with the cycles of vibration getting faster, you're moving the throttle in the wrong direction. As you get closer to being in synch, the cycles of vibration will slow down until they hum together. You can't mistake it: Both engines purring together exactly in tune with each other.

With an automatic synchronizer, one of the engines will be the "master." After engaging the synchronizer all you have to do is set that engine's throttle and the "slave" engine will automatically follow. Automatic synchronizers will work with manual, hydraulic, or pneumatic throttle controls. You can engage or disengage them at any speed. They are set up so that if they quit working for some reason, they automatically disengage rather than hunt for the right rpm.

If your boat doesn't come with automatic synchronizers, they are readily available as an after-market item. You can install one yourself if you're handy, but figure on taking a day to do it right. The convenience and speed at which this device works, adjusting the throttles even when the seas get rough, can soon justify the purchase.

Twin-prop boats also have twin rudders, and these require more care than a single rudder. A single rudder only has to be pointed straight when the wheel is centered. The rudders of a twin need to be adjusted so there is a small amount of toe-in, with each rudder turning in, usually between one and three degrees on each rudder. Rudders that are perfectly parallel when going straight ahead will not track true, requiring you to make small steering adjustments constantly. If the rudders are turned out to any extent, the steering will be erratic and every wave will set you off in a new direction. While this is not something that needs to be checked regularly, it is an important part of setting up your boat. If your rudders are not calibrated properly or if they get out of adjustment after hitting something, you'll quickly know about the problem.

CHAPTER 10

DIFFICULT CONDITIONS

Going boating isn't always like the glossy pictures in travel magazines. There are days with bad weather, storms that blow in after a postcard-perfect morning, and afternoon thunderstorms with gusts of wind and heavy rain. If the problem isn't weather, it might be a sand bar that isn't on the chart. You need to know what to do when things get tough.

There are three basic strategies you can use to deal with difficult conditions: Avoid them, minimize them, or deal with them.

Avoiding the difficulty is the best strategy, as long as you know where or when the difficulty will be. If you know that the bar at the river's mouth develops large standing waves during the flood tide, the best thing to do is keep track of the tides. Keep a tide table on your boat.

You can't avoid bad weather if you don't know it is coming. Before you go out, the very least you need to do is listen to the NOAA weather broadcast for your area. Write down the forecast and tuck your note in with the charts. Listen again a few hours later and see if the forecast has changed.

Weather forecasts are not always right, and there is no substitute for your own eyes to determine local weather. If you pay attention to the local weather patterns, you will learn what it means when the wind starts to blow out of the east and then back to the north.

Despite your best efforts at prevention, things can go wrong. You might wake up at your anchorage to see dark clouds on the horizon. A boat in the anchorage could come adrift and head in your direction. When unavoidable difficulties occur, move to the next strategy: minimize. If bad weather's heading for you, consider changing course, even if it means going miles out of your way. Get out your chart and see where you are relative to the problem and your destination.

You might consider heading back to your home port. But don't be so intent on getting home that you pass up a safe refuge. Even a strange harbor is preferable to the open water in bad weather. If making it to the nearest port means you don't get home that afternoon, so be it. Get home the next day—safely.

Sometimes you won't be able to find a harbor in time, however. When you are taking stock of your situation, locate your position on the chart. Note the direction of the wind, the direction of the swells or waves, and any tidal or river current. Estimate how long it will take for the weather to get to you and then look for an area of sheltered water where you can get in the lee of the wind and out of the big waves. An inlet, a cove—even a shallow sand bar—will break the force of big waves, providing you have enough water behind the bar.

Be careful when approaching shallow water. If there are big swells coming in, you could touch bottom when your boat is in a wave trough. This can be a jarring collision, much more intense than just running aground while going ahead at four knots. Pay close attention to the depths marked on your chart and compare the readings with what you are seeing on your depth sounder.

When going into shallow water, it's crucial to understand what your depth sounder is reading. Is it telling you how much water there is from the depth sounder's transducer, or is it telling you how much water there is beneath the lowest part of your boat? Maybe it's telling you the true depth. All of these readings are acceptable methods of calibrating your depth sounder. But you need to know which one you're reading. Most depth sounders can be calibrated to read any of these choices, so adjust it to read the way you prefer. Don't forget to tell your crew how your sounder is reading so they will know how much water is under the keel.

Once you get into the sheltered area, you will be glad you rehearsed deploying the anchor with your crew. If you are coming into a marina, be certain your crew knows what to do before you get to the pier or the mooring.

Another reason to get off the water when things turn bad is that when a boat is bouncing around and stirring up the fuel, it can loosen sediment in the bottom of the tank and possibly clog a filter. The engine can quit, putting you at the mercy of the waves. A boat without power will always end up lying beam-on to the waves, and roll severely. If a wave hits the side of the boat while it is rolled down, it could fill the cockpit, making the boat sit lower in the water and inviting another wave aboard. If that happens too often, you can lose your boat.

If you can't get to sheltered water or port in time and deep water is near, then heading to sea may be the best idea, especially if you have a bigger boat that can handle big waves. It's not the water that's the most dangerous element; it's all those rocks below and closer to shore. In deep water, there is no danger of running aground, and you can head the boat in a direction where the exposure to wind and wave action is least.

Navigating your boat in stormy seas has its own dangers,

and that subject is covered in the next chapter. Heading to sea to ride out a storm is not a decision to be taken lightly, but it can be the right one in certain circumstances.

If you can neither avoid nor minimize the difficulty you are facing, then you must move to the third strategy: Deal with it. Here's where practice and familiarity with your boat and its handling characteristics pay off bigtime.

Once you have made a decision, whatever it is, stick to it long enough to see it work. Only if you realize the decision was obviously wrong should you change tactics. Many emergencies, such as a weather front, develop slowly. But there are such things as rapid emergencies. A fast vessel crossing your bow on a collision course requires a decision *now*, not in a few minutes after you mull it over. If you are pooped by a following sea and the cockpit is filled with water, you need to do something *now*.

A fire on board is probably the worst kind of emergency you could experience. Not only might you lose your boat but you could be severely injured. You need to find the fire extinguishers and locate the source of the flame *now*.

A massive hole in the hull, perhaps caused by a high-speed collision with a log or a container, is another emergency in which you have no time to go over alternatives. The right thing must be done, *now*.

Because there are a limited number of emergencies that develop rapidly, it makes sense to prepare for them in the form of drills. Your crew should be familiar with the location and use of the fire extinguishers and the engine's fire suppression system. Proper operation of the propane solenoid and the valves on the tanks are vital to the survival of the boat. Propane is heavier than air, and small leaks can result in a pool of propane gas in the bilge. One spark can produce an explosion with devastating force.

Everyone needs to know how to shut off and start the engine and have enough familiarity with the boat at least to steer it with some degree of accuracy. Your boat's automatic bilge pump will have an override switch; show it to your crew and then go to the bilge pump's pick-up to show them how to clear it of debris. If you begin to take on water, the bilge can become full of trash, from cellophane wrappers to lost fishing lures. If these get to the bilge pump strainer, they can clog the intake.

If your boat has a manual, emergency bilge pump (and all boats should have a bilge pump that does not need electricity), demonstrate its function to your crew.

Everyone on board needs to know where the lifejackets are located, the location of the boat's emergency signaling gear, and how to operate the boat's VHF radio.

Some skippers make a short list of the safety-related items on board for everyone coming on board to understand. You will find that after going over your boat's emergency systems a dozen times, you are more familiar with them as well. In a true emergency you won't have time to think or decide. You will have to react, and the only way to be certain your reactions are right is through practice.

The three strategies for difficult situations are worth saying again: Avoid it; Minimize it; Deal with it.

CHAPTER 11

ROUGH WEATHER

While Mark Twain (who was a professional mariner) was absolutely correct when he said we couldn't do anything about the weather except discuss it, we still need to make plans with the weather in mind. We can do this through our knowledge of how weather systems work and our ability to produce accurate forecasts. But to take advantage of the full range of resources available, you need to be able to do more than merely tune in to the NOAA weather forecast on your boat's VHF.

Meteorology, the science of weather, can be broken down into two parts, observation and forecasting. Observation is just that: Look out the window, read the barometer, see which way the wind is blowing. You can use observation to verify and fine-tune a forecast, the other half of meteorology.

The forecast you hear from the NOAA broadcasts or read in the newspaper is the product of multiple observations made at weather stations throughout the region. There are short-term forecasts that give the expected weather in the next 6 to 24 hours, and long-term forecasts dealing with the weather one to seven days ahead. The farther ahead the forecast looks, the less accurate it will be.

Weather forecasts are also specific to the area they cover.

A weather forecast for Miami will only be of limited use to you as you plan for a Gulf Stream crossing. A forecast that covers all of southern Florida won't tell you if there are going to be thunderstorms in Tampa Bay that afternoon. The smaller the area covered by the forecast, and the less in the future the forecaster looks, the more you can depend on its accuracy.

Ultimately, however, the weather you are concerned about is the weather you are in. If the forecast is for light east winds but you are seeing gusty northerlies, then you have to be your own meteorologist. If you plan to take your boat out for more than a single day, where you will be either anchoring or traveling from one marina to another, a barometer is an important instrument. You can use either a traditional aneroid barometer with an analog dial that resembles a clock face or a digital barometer that will also tell you the rate of barometric change, which can be an important piece of information.

Whether you will be water-skiing a mile from the launch ramp or heading offshore to fish, one of the most important parts of your pre-departure preparation will be checking on the weather. If it's a weekend trip, start the Tuesday before. Make a note of the expected conditions and compare the forecasts from day to day. By Friday you should have a pretty good idea about the conditions on Saturday, and the short-range forecast Saturday morning will have a high probability of accuracy.

Once you have decided to launch the boat, on the basis of the pre-departure weather forecast, you then change into a different weather mode. You will be observing and analyzing your weather and making very short-range forecasts: What will the weather be like in 15 minutes? In an hour?

Because it is likely that no forecast is going to tell you the weather for your particular lake or destination that day, the basics of how weather systems work and how to read a weather chart. You don't need to be a professional meteorologist to be able to read a weather chart. The symbols are simple, and there aren't many to learn. You want a weather chart that covers as small an area as you can find, using information that is as recent as possible. A weather chart is generally not a forecast; rather, it's a report on how things are at the time the chart was prepared. If it is a forecast, that will be plainly spelled out on the chart.

There is a dizzying array of weather websites you can go to. The names and URLs change often, so any written information of that sort can rapidly become out of date. Websites connected with the National Oceanographic and Atmospheric Administration (NOAA) offer the greatest variety and are a taxpayer-funded government resource. While there are, periodically, efforts to eliminate this service, sponsored by for-profit businesses that sell weather information, the concerns of safety and access to publicly funded information have continued to make this information available.

The basics of how weather works are simple. Air tends to move from areas of higher pressure to areas of lower pressure. This moving air, or wind, carries and produces weather systems (such as cloud, and storms) and produces waves. Uneven heating of the air produces the differences in pressure; this temperature difference produces high and low pressure. High-pressure areas, broadly speaking are characterized by cool (or cold) air, clear skies, and air that is sinking down in the center and moving outwards. The wind of a high-pressure area is strongest away from the center.

Low-pressure areas are characterized by rising masses of

air and significant cloud cover. The temperature of the air is cool, or possibly a mix of warm and cool air. The strongest winds are in the center of the low pressure area.

Large moving air masses that are cooler or warmer than the air surrounding them (or the surface under them) are known as weather factories. The changes in temperature can produce (or cause to cease) rain, snow, wind, clouds or any other manifestation of weather.

The boundary of an air mass is called a front. If the air mass is a cold one, it is called a cold front. The border is marked on a weather map with a set with small triangles. A warm front is marked with small half-circles.

The passage of a cold front produces changes that can be rapid and sometimes dramatic. The barometric pressure will drop immediately before the front arrives, because the dense cold air is sliding in under the existing warm air and

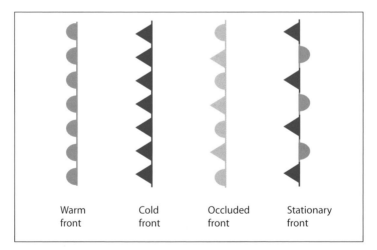

| Warm front | Cold front | Occluded front | Stationary front |

On weather maps, the side of the heavy line on which the symbols appear show which way the front is moving. There is no movement in a stationary front.

pushing it up. Once the front has arrived barometric pressure rises, often rapidly. The air temperature remains steady until the front passes, at which time it will again drop rapidly.

You can notice the position of the cold front by the presence of clouds, usually puffy cumulus. They will be fairly close to the actual front. You can also learn a lot by observing the wind patterns as well. Before the cold front arrives, watch for a wind shift from east-southeast to south-southwest. After the passage of the cold front, the wind will continue to veer in a clockwise direction to north-northwest.

A warm front comes with more fanfare than a cold front. Clouds precede it, sometimes by hundreds of miles. A warm front, containing warm and usually moist air, rides over the existing cooler and denser air, producing high-altitude cirrus clouds. As the front gets closer, the clouds get lower and there will usually be rain just before the front itself arrives. The rain can be heavy but will usually stop once the warm front passes.

Keep an eye on your barometer. You will notice the pressure dropping as the front approaches, becoming fairly stable once it passes. If the warm front is the leading edge of a deep low (usually with severe weather), the pressure could continue to drop.

The lines on a weather chart that connect areas of equal barometric pressure are called isobars. Just like the lines on a contour map, the closer the lines are to each other the steeper the pressure gradient. Because winds are the result of pressure differences, isobars that are close together are indicate of strong winds. In the northern hemisphere, winds going into the center of a low pressure zone flow in a counter-clockwise direction and winds coming out from a high-pressure zone flow in a clockwise direction.

Because we know the direction the wind moves, we use the wind's direction to tell us where the center of the low- (or high-) pressure area is located. Stand with your back to the wind and raise both arms up like a child playing airplane. Your left arm is now pointing at the center of the low-pressure area, and your right arm points to the center of the high.

The movement of cold and warm fronts can sometimes stop. It then becomes a stationary front and is symbolized by cold-front symbols on one side of the front and warm-front symbols on the other. There's not much change along a stationary front. Also, it's generally not the nicest of weather either, with rain and clouds lasting until the resumption of movement.

If a fast-moving cold front catches up and combines with a warm front, the result is an occluded front, symbolized by a line of cold- and warm-front symbols, but on the same side of the line. There will likely be rain on both sides of an occluded front. If you are on the west side, the winds will back, or change direction in counter-clockwise manner, beginning at east-southeast and moving eventually to north-northwest. On the east side of an occluded front, the winds will veer, or change in a clockwise direction, beginning at east-southeast and eventually to west-southwest or west-northwest.

Learn the symbols used on a weather chart to get the most from its information and alsounderstand how the information is arranged on a weather map's station plot. Weather stations send their information to a central point. This information is listed in a two- or three-line summary of numbers and symbols.

Your understanding of weather maps and what their symbols mean will allow you to get more information from a weather map. Knowing how the various elements of our weather interact will give you a better understanding and ability to provide your own weather forecast than you can get from any weather forecaster.

While being able to forecast the weather for your immediate area is a valuable skill, the minimum skill any boater needs is the ability to know the danger signs of approaching bad weather. The minimum basic weather reporting device on a boat is a barometer. This and an anemometer, which gives you wind speed and direction, will help you to make very good local predictions.

A rapidly falling barometer is a sure sign of trouble. If it is coupled with increasing wind speed and a continuing change in wind direction, you can be fairly certain that a low-pressure system is on the way. The rate of pressure drop is more indicative of the strength of the low than its distance or the time until its arrival.

Generally speaking, low-pressure systems move from west to east, although they can move in any direction. Easterlies and a falling barometer are generally signs of worsening weather, whereas a rising barometer and westerlies are generally a sign of fair or clearing weather.

If you have winds from the south or southeast with a steadily falling barometer, expect weather from the west or northwest. The center of the storm will likely pass to the north or nearby in 12 to 24 hours, at which time the wind will veer, or clock, first south, then southwest, and finally northwest.

East to northeast wind accompanied by a steadily falling barometer is evidence of a low-pressure system arriving from the south or southwest, with the center of the low passing near or to the south of you. The center will arrive 12 to 24 hours after detection and when it does, the wind will back north and then northwest.

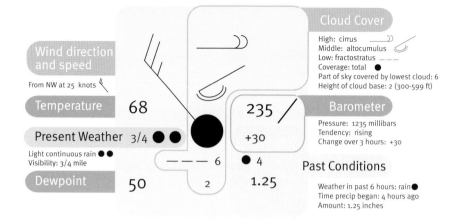

Wind direction and speed

From NW at 25 knots

Temperature 68

Present Weather 3/4

Light continuous rain ● ●
Visibility: 3/4 mile

Dewpoint 50

Cloud Cover

High: cirrus
Middle: altocumulus
Low: fractostratus _ _ _
Coverage: total ●
Part of sky covered by lowest cloud: 6
Height of cloud base: 2 (300-599 ft)

235 /
+30

Barometer

Pressure: 1235 millibars
Tendency: rising
Change over 3 hours: +30

● 4

_ _ _ 6

2   1.25

Past Conditions

Weather in past 6 hours: rain●
Time precip began: 4 hours ago
Amount: 1.25 inches

WEATHER MAP SYMBOLS

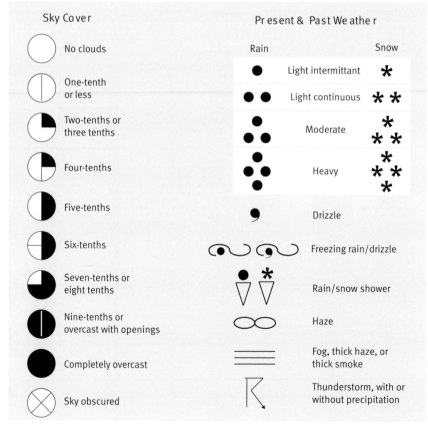

Sky Cover

- No clouds
- One-tenth or less
- Two-tenths or three tenths
- Four-tenths
- Five-tenths
- Six-tenths
- Seven-tenths or eight tenths
- Nine-tenths or overcast with openings
- Completely overcast
- Sky obscured

Present & Past Weather

Rain		Snow
●	Light intermittant	✱
● ●	Light continuous	✱ ✱
● ● ●	Moderate	✱ / ✱ ✱
● ● ● ●	Heavy	✱ ✱ / ✱ ✱ ✱ / ✱

- Drizzle
- Freezing rain/drizzle
- Rain/snow shower
- Haze
- Fog, thick haze, or thick smoke
- Thunderstorm, with or without precipitation

Wind Speed

Knots	Miles per hour
Calm	Calm
1-2	1-2
3-7	3-8
8-12	9-14
13-17	15-20
18-22	21-25
23-27	26-31
28-32	32-37
33-37	38-43
38-42	44-49
43-47	50-54
48-52	55-60
53-57	61-66
58-62	67-71
63-67	72-77
68-72	78-83
73-77	84-89

Cloud Cover

HIGH clouds

Fllaments of cirrus, or "mares' tales," scattered and not increasing

Dense cirrus in patches or twisted sheaves, usually not increasing, sometimes like remnants of cumulonimbus; or towers or tufts

Cirrus, often hook-shaped, gradually spreading over the sky and usually thickening as a whole

Cirrus and cirrostratus, often in converging bands, or cirrostratus alone; generally overspreading and growing denser

Cirrostratus not increasing and not covering entire sky

Middle clouds

Thin altostratus (most of cloud layer semi-transparent)

Thin altocumulus in patches; cloud elements continually changing and/or occuring at more than one level

Thin altocumulus in band or in a layer gradually spreading ove rthe sky and usually thickening as a whole

Altocumulus of a chaotic sky, usually at different levels; patches of dense cirrus are usually present also

Low clouds

Cumulus of fair weather, little vertical development, and seemingly flattened

Cumulus of considerable development, generally towering, with or without either cumulus or stratocumulus bases all at the same level

Stratocumulus formed by spreading out of cumulus; cumulus often present also

Cumulonimbus having a clearly fibroud (cirroform) top, often anvil-shaped, with or withoutcumulus, stratocumulus, stratus or scud

A rising barometer is generally indicative of fair weather, and a barometer that reads 1020 Mb or higher, with the reading either steady or slowly rising, foretells good weather for the next 24 hours. If the weather has been unsettled and then the barometer suddenly rises 1030 Mb or more, things are going to get better fairly soon.

A rapid change in the barometer, whether up or down, usually indicates strong winds that will begin very soon. But high winds are not necessarily accompanied by a change in the barometer. If the system is stalled, with a stationary front, the winds may blow for some time without any significant change in pressure. The isobars can be close together, indicating a steep pressure gradient, but if the centers of the low or high aren't moving, neither is the barometer.

Consider the opposite case: a rapid fall of the barometer, but no wind. That signifies a fast-moving low or high, but without a steep pressure gradient. The isobars are far apart, but the system centers are moving rapidly. The wind's speed and direction, as well as the barometric pressure, all have to be taken into consideration when you are visualizing what will happen in your weather neighborhood.

Public warning systems can be an important source of weather information as well. Different warning categories are provided on the radio when high winds and rough weather are forecast. They are also sometimes displayed as flags and lights. If high winds and rough weather are forecast, the flags and lights of tradition may still be visible at some Coast Guard stations, yacht clubs, and marinas, although that practice has been formally discontinued for nearly 20 years. A single triangular red flag or a red light above a white light is a small craft advisory. There is no legal definition of what constitutes a small craft, but this

Above right is an aneroid barometer. A barometer is the minimum basic weather reporting device on a boat: a rising barometer generally means fair weather is ahead, and a rapidly falling barometer signals bad weather's on its way.

warning indicates weather conditions in the coastal and nearshore waters that exceed previously defined thresholds that are specific to geographic areas. Higher winds are more acceptable in protected waters than they are in open water, for example. Wind speeds, depending on the area, can range from 20 to 33 knots to trigger a small craft warning.

A gale warning is a forecast for winds 34 to 47 knots. The visual warning for this is two triangular red flags or a white light above a red light, and it is a notch above a small craft advisory in the severity of conditions forecast.

A storm warning is a forecast of winds above 48 knots, with no upper limit. The visual day signal is a single storm flag: a square red flag with a black square in the center. The night signal is two red lights, one above the other. If the storm-force winds are associated with a hurricane or a cyclone, however, the storm warning signal or notification indicates winds in the range of 48 to 63 knots.

A hurricane day signal is two stacked storm flags and the night signal is three, stacked lights: red, white and red.

A hurricane warning is a forecast for winds greater than 64 knots in conjunction with a hurricane. It is not the same thing as a hurricane watch, which is an announcement that a hurricane is near enough so that residents and mariners should keep informed of current weather developments in case a hurricane warning is issued.

	Small Craft Advisory	Gale Warning	Storm Warning	Hurricane Warning
	winds to 33 knots/ 38 mph	winds 34 - 47 knots/ 39 - 54 mph	winds 48 - 63 knots/ 55- 73 mph	winds above 64 knots/ 74 mph
DAY FLAGS red ▯ ▶ black ■				
NIGHT LIGHTS red ● white ●				

The National Weather Service no longer uses warning flags and lights, but some marinas and yacht clubs display them.

There is rarely a valid reason for anyone to go out when there is a small craft advisory. The advisory covers not just sustained winds but also gusts and wave conditions. Regardless of the size of your boat, it won't be comfortable. If you are already out on the water and you hear a small craft advisory on the radio, give serious thought to heading in, finding a harbor or preparing your boat and crew for weather. A small craft warning can occur any time—in fact, if you spend enough time on the water, you will be out when one is issued. Take stock of your boat and crew: are they experienced hands that have been out in 30 knots of wind before? Is your boat capable of dealing safely with large waves? Most important, are *you* capable of dealing with high winds and big waves? In an open boat, with waves kicking up higher than your boat's freeboard, you may be only one or two waves away from being swamped.

As for hurricanes and tropical storms, these days there are warnings literally days ahead of a hurricane's expected arrival in any given area. In most cases, that gives you time to pull your boat from the water or secure it with doubled dock lines and cleared topsides.

Any boater who has survived being on the water during a severe storm will tell you that the best cure is prevention.

CHAPTER 12

ROUGH SEAS

L ike bad weather, rough seas are a fact of a boater's life. If you spend enough time on the water, you will experience both. Waves caused by wind are the main cause of rough seas. The size of the waves generated by winds is determined by three factors: the strength of the wind, how long the wind has been blowing, and the "fetch," the distance upwind to the nearest land.

On the open ocean, there are also swells to contend with. Whereas waves are caused by wind and move in the same direction as the wind, swells are the result of distant storms or weather. The many waves generated by that storm eventually join together and become swells, which move without regard to the wind direction. When the wind blows in a different direction from swells, the result can be difficult seas.

If a storm blows long enough to set up wave trains, and then the winds change direction, the cross seas can be especially treacherous. Add in yet a third wind change, and you have confused seas that are maddening to steer through.

To understand how to handle waves, let's look at how a wave works. If we cut a wave into a cross section, we see the crest, or top, and the trough, or low part, of the wave. A given molecule of water rotates in a circle as the wave passes. This rotational movement of water extends below the wave for a distance of only about one-half the wavelength, or the distance from one crest to the next.

When this rotating mass of water gets into water that is too shallow for the bottom part to rotate freely, there's only one place for the energy to go: up. The wave gets higher and higher until it is too high to stand up, and then the top falls over, as the wave breaks. Breaking waves can be seen on any coast.

If you are in a train of deep ocean swells that have been generated by storms hundreds of miles away, the swells can be a hundred feet or more from crest to crest. These swells can touch bottom in 50 feet of water and generate towering, breaking waves in 30 feet of water, perhaps a mile or more from shore. When the waves start to break because of the bottom, their forward motion is slowed. Waves are, in essence, nothing more than energy being kicked from one water molecule to another. The energy of a wave remains pretty much the same until it hits the shore and finally disintegrates, so if the wave starts to slow down, and the bottom of it is being pinched off by the ocean floor, the wave gets higher. When a wave is affected by shallower water, it is said to be shoaling. When the fast-moving top part of the wave falls over the decelerating bottom part (caused by the rapidly diminishing water depth) you get a breaker.

Because waves need water under them to form fully, storms in shallow bodies of water can produce waves with steep leading edges. These waves break more readily and can be very difficult to navigate because of the short distance between their crests.

Offshore, or in water deep enough where the bottom has no effect, waves generally break either because they get too steep or because the wind blows off their crests. A wave's forward motion means that the leading part of the crest is generally steeper than the trailing part, and the crests are steeper than the troughs. A boat that gets caught beam-on to a large wave can be put at a steep enough angle that it can roll. The crest can break against the hull and fill the boat with water or tumble it down the face of the wave.

As we said earlier, eventually even the most careful boater is likely to get caught in heavy seas. If the waves are beginning to pick up and the winds have been blowing, then it's time to take a cool assessment of your situation. The chances are very good that you will be able to navigate your boat through the seas and get home with nothing more than a good sea story, but you need to remain in

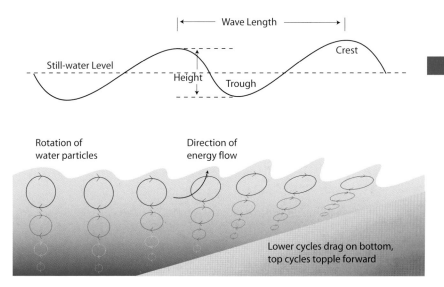

When rotating wave molecules get into water too shallow for the bottom part to rotate freely, the energy builds the wave up until it topples over.

charge of your boat and yourself. This is the wrong time for panic, as you need to steer your boat with a sure hand.

The first thing to do is make sure all the hatches, portlights, and doors are closed and secured. Next, pump the bilges dry and keep them that way. Water sloshing around in the bilges can have a destabilizing effect on your boat.

Be certain that everything on board is secured. Tie down or stow any loose items, whether they are plates in the galley or fishing gear.

Before it gets too rough, have the crew put on their lifejackets. While you have the crew's attention, brief them on what's happening, reassure them, and assign each member some task, if possible. A busy crew will have less of a problem with seasickness.

Determine your location and make plans for getting to your harbor. A few notes on compass headings and distances are much easier to read than a chart. If you have to stay at sea, make sure you have enough sea room to motor in the direction dictated by the waves and wind, assuming that you are more concerned with easing the ride than getting ashore.

You may discover that it's impossible to go in the direction you need for destination A. Having a destination B can be a lifesaver; notes on headings and distance should be part of your preparation.

The direction you go relative to the motion of the waves is the critical aspect of heavy weather navigation. Regardless of your motion relative to that of the waves, match your speed to the conditions: The worse the weather, the slower you will go.

Running into the waves, or head seas, can be wet and challenging, but this is generally the preferred angle of attack. If the waves become too steep or large, you may find it best to slow down and change your angle to the waves to more like 45 degrees. You can reduce forward speed to practically zero, holding your position in the water and riding over each wave as it comes. Steer up the face, over the crest, and into the calmer water on the back side, only to do it all over again. You may find that the boat will hold itself in the water in a fairly comfortable manner if you stop the forward motion and just hold the boat in place. The waves will hit the bow with the least force, and you will go just fast enough to provide steering. If you need to make a large change of direction to meet a wave, do it with a lot of rudder and a hard hit of the throttle.

The propeller can come out of the water, especially as you crest the wave. Avoid this as much as possible, to keep control of your boat. Steering through heavy seas will require constant steering and continual attention to the throttle. Each boat has its own characteristics, although all boats are better off meeting seas bow-on rather than beam-on.

Trim adjustment can be very important. The bow has to be high enough to rise above the waves rather than plow through them but not so high that it slews to one side. Take each wave as it comes, work your way up the clean part of the wave, and avoid the steep combers. If a really big wave is in front of the boat, slow down so that the wave passes under you. A generous application of throttle will give you steering from the prop wash.

Forget about maintaining a straight course in these conditions. While you may make progress to your destination, the important thing is to survive each wave as it comes. Keep the engine driving the prop, and don't let the boat lose steerage.

If your course requires you to run parallel to the waves, you won't be able to spend your entire time in the troughs of the waves. When you begin to go up the face of the wave, steer into it. A wiser choice, when confronted with beam seas, might be to make a series of tacks, just as a sailboat does.

Turn so that you first take the wind and waves on the bow. After you tack, you will have the wind and waves on the forward quarter as you take them at 45 degrees off the bow. Depending on your destination, the set of the waves, and the direction of the wind, one tack or the other will take you to your destination more quickly. You may be within 25 degrees of the desired course on one tack but 60 degrees from your desired course on the other. Once you have determined which tack is best, favor that one as you make your way through the waves. The tack with the wind and waves on the bow will probably be the more comfortable one, and a small change in your heading on either tack can make a significant difference in your comfort and the distance to your destination.

Don't make too many tacks, however, which can be dangerous. Get each tack over with as quickly as possible. Let the boat slow down in the trough. Back off the throttle and then turn the wheel hard over in the new direction. Give a strong hit of throttle so the prop wash will hit the rudder and push the stern over, so the bow is in the new direction. Straighten the wheel and get moving on the new tack.

If you have to run before the seas, be aware that this can be the most difficult and potentially dangerous angle. The problems can begin when your boat crests a wave and begins to slide down the face. As the boat goes over the crest and descends the face of the wave, the prop and then part of the rudder come out of the water.

If the rudder loses its grip and the stern begins to yaw because of the wave action, you may lose control of the boat. The stern can slew around so the boat is beam-on to the wave and your boat can broach, be tossed into the trough of the wave with you unable to steer the boat. The boat will probably roll to windward initially, down the face of the wave. If the boat rights itself, the rudder may suddenly bite and the boat will suddenly turn, placing the other side of the boat to windward as it rolls even more severely. After doing this once or twice, boats have been known to roll right over.

Broaching must be avoided at all costs. It is the greatest single danger to your boat when in rough seas. Avoidance tactics include reducing boat speed so the seas pass under the boat and reducing the engine speed so the engine doesn't labor when running into a wave and run free when the boat picks up speed at the crest. Stay ahead of the boat's

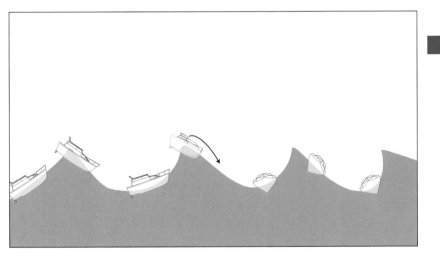

If the rudder loses its grip and the stern begins to yaw because of the wave action, the stern can slew around so the boat is beam-on to the wave. The boat can broach – be tossed onto the trough of the wave with you unable to steer. Broaching must be avoided at all costs.

motion and use only enough throttle to maintain steerage.

You can also use the same tactic suggested earlier for dealing with beam seas: Tacking will allow you take the following seas on the stern quarter rather than directly onto the transom. This will greatly reduce the tendency of the stern to yaw. The same strategies used to change direction when tacking upwind can be used when tacking down wind: Slow down, turn the wheel, hit the throttle, and move off in the new direction.

The confused seas resulting from a major change in wind direction are best dealt with by reducing speed and trying to determine which set of swells is dominant. Steer to that set, if possible, while working your way around the other waves.

The phenomenon of the so-called "rogue wave" is not the result of too many days at sea or a hyperactive imagination. A rogue wave is, basically, a wave that is significantly larger than any other wave in the area. One theory behind the rogue wave requires a little understanding of waves themselves. If you were to draw a set of waves, you would have a series of more or less equal up and down curves. If you drew another set of waves with the peaks farther apart, and then placed this drawing on top of the first one, you would see that at certain places the peaks of both sets of waves were together. At another point the peaks of one set were exactly over the troughs of the other.

When two sets of waves cross each other's path in the ocean, and when the peaks coincide, you get an extra-high wave. When the peak coincides with a trough, you would get an extra-low wave. If several sets of waves all happened to have their peaks coincide, then you would get a rogue wave.

Another popular theory explains rogue waves as the result of ocean swells colliding with ocean currents, sometimes combined with sea-bottom profiles, to produce a

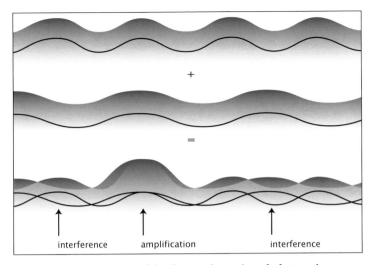

interference   amplification   interference

One theory of rogue waves explains them as the product of a fast-moving wave series (top) combining with a larger, slow-moving series (middle), producing an unusually large wave (bottom.)

wave of uniquely immense size. The final contender in the rogue wave theory contest explains them as the product of a fast-moving wave train catching up to and combining with a larger, slower-moving wave train. If this also happens in water shallow enough so that the wave touches bottom, an unusually large wave can result. Remember that a water depth less than half the distance between crests will affect a wave, and a big swell can be hundreds of feet between crests.

The bottom line is that rogue waves are rare, cannot be forecast, and only last for a short time. Worrying about them will do nothing to lessen their danger. They are more common than meteorite strikes, probably more common than we had thought, but they are not something you need to worry about, if only because of their rarity, essentially unpredictable nature and tendency to occur well offshore.

If you are in rough seas and you have a boat designed for the task, have faith in your boat and your own skill. While you might not want to head out in the middle of a gale to practice your storm tactics, practicing your wave navigation methods and steering tactics can be done any time there is a heavy swell running.

If you have an open boat, head for shore before the wind gets up. The less ability your boat has to deal with big waves, the more alert you need to be for weather changes. No amount of skill will promise salvation of a 15-foot runabout in gale-force winds. As the skipper of the boat, regardless of its size, you are personally responsible for the lives and safety of everyone on board. Any old salt will tell you that it is always better to be in the harbor glad you're not on the water than out there wishing you were back in the harbor.

The last type of rough seas you might encounter are at the entrance to a harbor where a sand bar has been built up. This causes waves when the outgoing tide meets incoming wave sets. Even at slack high water, the waves can break uncomfortably because of the shoaling bottom. The waves may not be easily seen from sea, because the foam from the breakers will be on the shore-side of the wave. The face of the breaking wave will be very steep, and the wave motion can change the location and size of the sand bar fairly quickly. The channel markers may not necessarily be in the deepest water, depending on how recently they have been moved. If you are unfamiliar with the inlet, make a radio call and get some local knowledge about the area.

Watch the waves as they approach the inlet. Generally the deepest water will be where the waves are the smallest. The waves will be lower on a flood tide, so waiting for the tide to turn can be part of your strategy.

While you're standing off, carefully observe the waves. They will usually run in sets of three, sometimes more, and the last of the set will be the biggest. You want to come in behind (on the back of) that last big wave. As you enter, keep your speed down to match that of the wave. Don't let the boat speed down the face of the wave; when the boat reaches the trough, the bow can dig in and the boat can be pitchpoled, or thrown end over end, with disastrous results.

You need to watch the waves in front and behind. A large wave could build and come in over the transom if you neglect to give a touch of throttle to get ahead of it.

Once you enter the inlet, you are committed to finish the job. You won't be able to turn around or make major changes of direction, so be sure of your decision. Again, careful observation from outside the inlet will help you in planning your tactics.

The whole topic of rough seas can sound intimidating, but as we mentioned at the beginning, you will almost certainly experience them at some time. If you pay attention to the weather and your location, the danger presented by the waves will be lessened. Just as with any other potential problem on the water, prevention is much better than cure.

CHAPTER 13

GROUNDING

People who don't get out on the water don't understand how experienced boaters become grounded. They think that because you know how much water it takes to float the boat, and the charts tell you how deep the water is, you should never run aground. Unfortunately, it is not a perfect world.

Currents and waves can carry sediment into navigable channels; a series of thunderstorms can fill streams with mud that ends up in your harbor. After a tropical storm passes through, be especially careful the first few times you go out. Hurricanes can make significant changes in the bottom profile, inlets, islands, and bays.

Even with all these natural and normal changes in water depth, it is probably safe to say that most groundings are the result of skipper error, often compounded by poor visibility. So most groundings are preventable. If you watch your chart, slow down, and avoid unfamiliar areas after sundown, lessen your chance of running aground.

Knowing how to read a chart is the first and most basic skill any boater needs before heading out. The standard reference to decipher marine charts is US Chart Number One, which resembles a small magazine rather than a chart. If you don't carry one on board, you should at least have one at home.

The depths are plotted with lines that connect places with the same water depth. Because oceans are tidal, the depths listed are in reference to the amount of water you can expect at mean low water or some other tidal condition and stage. This variable will be noted in the legend. Depths are marked in feet, meters, or fathoms, and the units used will be noted on the chart, usually in large letters. Because of the way the depth is calculated, you can nearly always count on having at least the charted depth of water and often more.

If the body of water is a fresh water lake or reservoir, the depths will be given relative to a stated reference. Before you leave, note the variation between charted depths and the reference depth. If the chart says marked depths are with a pool or lake level of 600 feet above sea level. If the body of water is a fresh water lake or reservoir, the depths will be given relative to a stated reference. Before you leave, note the variation between charted depths and the reference depth. If the chart says marked depths are with a pool or lake level of 600 feet above sea level, then any variation from that will affect the actual depth. This information will usually be available at the marina, or it may be posted at the launching ramp. In the example above, a pool level of 580 feet would reduce all charted depths by 20 feet.

Every boat too large to be pushed off a sand bar by a sole skipper should have a depth sounder. Some handheld depth sounders look like small flashlights. Many boaters on small, open boats find these to be the right tool to find underwater structures like ledges or canyons where fish hide.

The depth sounder on a bigger boat requires calibrating for proper use. The readout can give you one of three versions of the water depth: It can tell you how much water there is between the transducer and the bottom; it can tell

On a navigational chart, depths are marked in feet, meters, or fathoms. Places with the same water depth are shown with connecting lines.

you how much water there is under the keel of the boat, or it can tell you how much water there is from the surface to the bottom. The selection is up to you, but the difference can be crucial.

Take note of where the transducer is located. If it is too far forward, it would be out of the water some of the time. Because most planing hulls ride very bow-high at slow speeds, the transducer is located halfway back along the hull, or sometimes even in the stern.

♟ Famous Flubs ≡

Will has been taking fishing very seriously for several years now, ever since he was able to take early retirement. Combining pensions with his wife, he was able to move down to Big Pine Key, where the couple lived in the vacation house Will's family had used for years. The first thing he did after the move was to buy a new Contender 23 and set it up for fishing.

"We had gone out to Little Spanish Key to do some fishing and after it got dark we decided to move over to Spanish Banks," Will said, "There's a long shallow area just north of the key where I had always had good luck on previous trips. We pulled up the anchor and I motored slowly for about a mile and a half until the GPS said we were in the right place. I was getting ready to put the anchor over the side when we heard a series of big splashes just off the bow.

"I put it in gear and moved slowly over to where the splashing had happened and pretty soon I felt the keel touching bottom. I looked at the depth gauge and it said we had enough water so I turned the wheel to the left, where I thought it was a bit deeper.

"I felt the boat hit the bottom again and figured it was just a little ridge since the depth gauge still said we had enough water. I gave it a bit of gas and we moved another few feet; it seemed to be clear of the bottom so I gave it another bit of gas." Will smiled at the memory, a bit of a funny smile.

"We got moving with enough speed to steer the boat and I thought we were out of the shallow stuff. Then we stopped. It was a slow-motion kind of stop, and I could feel the bow riding up on the mud. I put it in reverse. Nothing. I wiggled the wheel back and forth, shifted forward and reverse. Nothing. I turned to the guys, 'Well, I guess we're here,' I said."

While his buddies made a few jokes, they got busy fishing. Will let them get on with it and then he had a look at the tide tables.

"I ran down to our date and then looked at the times. 'High tide 8:06 p.m.' it said. Then I had a look at my watch. It was just past 11:00 p.m.," and the tide was within this much of high water," said Will, measuring six inches with his thumb and forefinger.

The first rule of running aground is to only do it at low water on the flood so the incoming tide will float you off. Whatever you do, don't run aground at high tide. This is what Will had just done. Every minute his boat had less water around it, and within an hour they were stuck enough so that the boat quit rocking with the waves.

Will took a longer look at the tide table. He saw that there was another, much higher high tide following this tide, and that the tide was going to turn in an hour. "After the tide turned it was going to come in fast because that high tide was two feet higher than this one," he said. "I figured we would be able to get off an hour or two after the turn."

An hour into the flood the boat was still stuck and his buddies had quit making jokes. They wanted to get moving and didn't want to wait around for the tide.

"We rocked the boat back and forth. I had them stand on one side and then the other while I gunned the engine, but I didn't want to suck too much dirt into the engines so we stopped," he said. "I told the guys they were going to have to get out and walk," he said with a chuckle.

"With everybody off the boat it was almost floating so we pushed it back and then sideways into water where it floated. Good thing that boat doesn't take too much water to float," he said.⚓

Most depth sounders allow you to set a shallow-water alarm at a depth of your choosing. When you get into water shallower than the preset amount, the alarm goes off. If you decide to set the alarm, don't set it so the alarm goes off 15 seconds before you run aground.

Let's analyze what Will did in this grounding. The first correct thing he did, after he ran aground, was to get out the tide tables. That information will determine what you do in the near future. If the tide has turned and is on the flood, the chances are you won't be stuck for very long. If, like Will and his friends, you end up aground with the tide on its way out, you either have to work very fast or decide you like it where you are.

If the tidal range is large, your boat can end up literally high and dry. If you have a boat with high deadrise, you need to be concerned with the boat listing to one side or the other, which could complicate things when the tide begins to come in. You might have to brace the boat against falling over or close windows and doors against waves.

Will's decision to quit revving the engine when the boat was firmly aground was a good one. Cooling water, whether fresh or salt, that is filled with sand and mud can clog filters, abrade water pumps, and cause premature wear throughout the engine. The prop, spinning in mud, can be damaged or become worn on the leading edge, spoiling its shape and reducing its efficiency.

The cure for Will's boat being aground was twofold. He and his crew waited until the tide turned and began to raise the water level, and then they reduced the boat's displacement by stepping out of the boat. Fortunately the water around the Florida Keys is warm and the boat didn't draw a lot of water. A boat that needs, say, five feet of water wouldn't be as easy to push round, with water possibly near head level on some of the crew. A larger boat wouldn't have its draft reduced as much by the expedient of the crew stepping overboard, either.

The location of the transducer told Will he had water underneath the sending unit, but because the bottom wasn't flat the boat was hung up on an unmeasured part.

Not all groundings end as simply as Will's. Hitting a sand bar or mud bank at high speed can damage a boat's hull, perhaps enough so that the boat will not be seaworthy, even if the tide comes in enough to float the boat off the shoal. Passengers can also be hurt. If the boat hits rocks, the impact is much more severe. The crew can be injured or thrown out.

Inland waters, like harbors, lakes, or the Intracoastal Waterway, don't betray the presence of shallow water as readily as open water does, because the waves are smaller. In the daytime you can see differences in color, but at night you may not realize you are running out of water until you feel the keel touching the bottom, especially if the bottom is shoaling rapidly. You may run aground at practically the same moment the depth sounder warns you of shallow water.

Another problem with running at high speed when the water depth is not certain is that the depth sounder doesn't work well at high speeds. The bubbles will interfere with the sonic pulses and the readings will exhibit random errors.

In any area where you have concerns about water depth, keep one eye on the chart and the other on the water ahead. Keep your speed down and watch the color of the water ahead. Polarized sunglasses will reduce the glare and help you see below the water's surface.

The advent of small, reliable, and inexpensive chart plotters, with screens that are visible in daylight, has revolutionized navigation. Even small boats can equip themselves with a unit that will display the boat's location superimposed on a chart of the area. Some chart plotters will allow you to customize the display, setting off all areas that are too shallow for your boat in a different color. You can plot routes that avoid those places simply by entering waypoints.

Chart plotters can't think for you. If you enter two waypoints with a shallow area in between them, the plotter will simply send you on a straight line between the two waypoints. So after you enter your waypoints, go over the points in between to be certain there is nothing there to hamper navigation.

If you are motoring along and suddenly see the water changing color and it looks like you are heading into shallow waters, slow down. Send someone to the bow to serve as a lookout. Remind your lookout to hold on in case you run aground.

When you feel the boat begin to touch bottom, it's time to back up. Don't use a lot of throttle in case there are obstructions on the bottom that may damage the prop. If you are solidly aground and there are waves pushing the boat further onto the shoal, setting an anchor may prevent you going further up on the sand bar.

If you've hit something solid, check for hull damage. If the hull has been holed and water is coming in faster than you can deal with, you may not want to get free. You'll sink in deeper water. Stay put and call for help.

If you're not in immediate danger of losing the boat and there are no serious injuries, a Mayday call is not appropriate. Get on channel 16 (or the dedicated channel for Sea Tow or the local towing service) and explain the nature of your problem. Give your precise location, using either the coordinates or a precise description with reference points.

Before you are towed off, you may need to do a quick repair of the hole. Make the towboat operators aware of the problem, and they will stop the leak enough to get you safely to a repair facility onshore.

The tow line needs to be attached to a strong cleat on the boat. If the tow requires a lot of pulling, it may be necessary to pass a towing line around the entire boat. If you have two bow cleats, you can attach the line to both of them, perhaps with a bridle, to spread the load.

Once you've been pulled free, go over the boat for dam-

Depth sounders and chart plotters such as the ones shown above are reliable tools and have become inexpensive enough for virtually every boater.

age. Check that the steering works properly by turning the wheel fully in both directions and checking that the rudder, stern drives, or outboard also turn fully. Check that the prop is clear and free to rotate. Engage the transmission and verify that the prop turns freely, without vibration. The prop may have been damaged and you may still need the services of the towboat.

Be aware of the technical difference between a tow and a salvage. Towing is generally taken to mean one towboat, one tow line, and the absence of peril to life. If you don't have to accept the first offer of help then it is probably a tow. Towing is charged for by the hour, generally beginning when the towboat leaves the dock and ending when the towboat returns to the dock. Often the price for the tow will be settled via the radio when you make contact with the service.

Salvage, on the other hand, implies an immediate peril to life, whether due to a holed hull, fire, or being hard aground. If the operation requires more than one rescue vessel or imperils other vessels or the marine environment, then it is salvage, not towing. If your rescue involves special equipment like pumps or flotation gear for your boat, or it includes being towed from the site, that, too, is salvage. Be aware beforehand which it is, as the bill for salvage can be much higher.

Before you take a tow line, find out whether it is a tow or salvage. A fixed-price salvage (or tow) is preferable, and we would advise against signing a "Lloyd's Open Form Salvage Contract." BoatUS, the Society of Maritime Arbitrators, and the Miami Maritime Arbitration all have forms that are based on the Lloyd's contract. If a contract is needed, these are preferable. If you and the salvor can't agree to a written contract, try to establish verbally a price for the operation in front of a witness.

You don't have to have a signed agreement for the salvor

to make a claim. They only have to prove that the rescue was successful and voluntary, and that your boat, crew, or the marine environment was in immediate peril.

If you sign an open form salvage contract the cost will be determined later and will result in a salvage lien being assigned against your boat.

If your boat sinks in navigable waters, you are liable for the removal of the wreck and will be assessed costs related to environmental damage and hazardous material removal.

Calling the Coast Guard is not an option unless there is immediate danger to life. If they show up and decide it is beyond their ability to salvage your boat, you can select the company to do the salvage.

If you're getting a tow from a friend or someone near by, be sure of what is being offered. Any salvor, whether professional or otherwise, can make a salvage claim if the circumstances warrant. Contrary to dockyard rumors, it makes no difference whether you use their tow line or yours. A verbal agreement, with witnesses, is usually sufficient. If you're not comfortable with the arrangement, call a commercial towing service.

From all the above, it stands to reason that your boat insurance policy needs to be specific as to coverage for towing and salvage. If you do end up in front of a marine arbitration board, you want someone on your side.

If you offer to tow another boat, rest assured that you will not be held liable for civil damages resulting from assistance to another boat if that service is asked for and given freely. The unwritten law of the sea says that you are to offer assistance to any vessel in peril, and the 1971 Federal Boating Safety Act has a Good Samaritan clause that protects boaters who act in good faith as reasonable and prudent fellow mariners to provide for or arrange towing, medical care, or other assistance.

CHAPTER 14

EMERGENCY SITUATIONS

D espite your best efforts, emergencies can and do happen. A boat is a bouncy, unstable place to do such activities as cleaning fish, changing clothes or even walking. As a responsible skipper, you need to be prepared for emergencies and deal with them to prevent things from getting worse.

The most basic preparation for medical emergencies is a first-aid kit. The longer you are going to be away from professional medical care, whether you figure that distance in time or miles, the more thought you need to give to your first-aid kit. If you are never more than a few miles from shore on an inland lake with a hospital relatively near, your first-aid kit will be pretty basic.

Rather than trying to figure out what you need based on the number of passengers, how far you will be from medical help, and how long the trip will last, just follow professional advice.

A home medical kit is designed to take care of the kinds of cuts and scrapes that kids get. For anything more serious, even someone with a big medical kit is going to call 911. It's easier than one might like to think for relatively serious injuries to happen on a boat.

The kit should be easy to use, designed for boaters, and kept in a waterproof case. Rather than go into detail about what to take for an afternoon of pulling the kids on water toys versus what to take if you're going across the Gulf Stream for two weeks in the Bahamas, we suggest going to the experts. Two companies that provide professionally designed medical kits for boaters are Adventure Medical Kits (www.adventuremedicalkits.com) and First Aid Pak (www.firstaidpak.com).

The Coast Guard doesn't require for first-aid kits if your boat doesn't carry paying passengers. But if you need a good standard for your medical kit, regardless of the supplier, look for a kit that meets or exceeds the Coast Guard's minimum requirements for small passenger vessels as listed in 46 CFR 121.710 and 184.710.

No boating emergency has the same level of immediacy as fire. There is nowhere to go; help is, practically speaking,

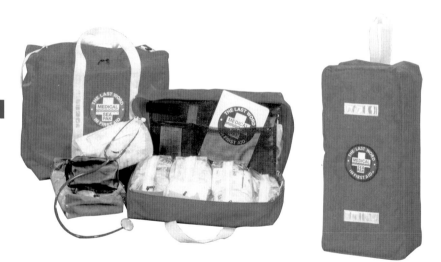

Onboard first-aid kits should be customized for the length of voyage and the cruising waters. Long-range offshore cruisers require more extensive first-aid supplies and lifesaving equipment than day and weekend boaters.

unavailable; and, because nearly everything on a boat is flammable, a small fire can become a big one very quickly.

Fire extinguishers will be checked by the Coast Guard when they board your boat. If you have an outboard engine without permanently mounted fuel tanks, and your boat is less than 26 feet long, you don't need a fire extinguisher to pass a Coast Guard inspection. A powerboat of any size that has permanent fuel tanks, an enclosed living space, or an enclosed engine compartment must carry fire extinguishers: one, two or three, depending on the length of your boat. In practice, the USCG minimums are just that, and you should select the number and location of your boat's fire extinguishers based on your boat's layout and equipment. If your boat has a motor, you need a fire extinguisher.

One extinguisher should be in the cockpit and one in the galley, located where you can reach it if the stove catches fire. Every cabin should have a fire extinguisher. A small, two-pound fire extinguisher rated 5 BC will run out of extinguishing material in less than 10 seconds and a 10BC-rated extinguisher with 2.75 pounds of extinguisher will last only a few seconds longer. If you have a fire and only carry the USCG minimum, you could run out of fire extinguisher in less than 30 seconds. If you have an engine in an enclosed compartment, give serious thought to installing a fixed extinguisher with an automatic heat-activated trigger and a manually activated backup switch.

Extinguishers are rated according to the type of fire they will put out. "A" extinguishers are good only for wood, paper, rubber or fiberglass fires. "B" extinguishers are good for flammable liquids, such as fuel, alcohol, kerosene, paint, and so on. "C" fires are electrical fires—shut off the electricity and these will probably become "A" fires. "D" fires are caused by flammable metals magnesium, not likely to occur on a boat. The ratings are linear; a 10BC extinguisher is twice as effective as a 5BC.

The Coast Guard rates fire extinguishers by the weight of extinguishing material and classification of fire. "B" means the unit is suitable for extinguishing flammable liquids. Under five pounds gets a B-I rating: a 10-pound extinguisher has a B-II rating, without regard to the type of fire for which each is designed.

If you have a fire, aim the extinguisher at the base of the fire and sweep the spray back and forth. You don't have long; even if you have a dozen extinguishers, a boat is a small place and you will either put out the fire quickly or have to abandon ship.

We highly recommend practicing with a fire extinguisher. Even if you don't use it to put out a fire, just seeing how long it lasts, the size of the stream, and its range will give you valuable experience if you ever have to use it. The local USCG Auxiliary or the US Power

Fire extinguishers are classified according to their extinguishing capacity and the type of fire for which they're suitable. Letters indicate the type of fire (wood, gasoline, electric, combustible metals). Numbers indicate capacity: the higher the number, the greater the capacity.

Squadrons chapter may periodically have fire-training days. These will provide you with an excellent opportunity to put out a fire under supervision by trained personnel.

You must carry emergency signaling devices, termed "visual distress signals" by the Coast Guard, on your boat if it is more than 16 feet long. Boats less than 16 feet long operated at night must still have night signaling devices. These devices include flares, both handheld and shot from a flare launcher, smoke signals, dye markers, signaling mirrors, electric lights with a programmed Morse code SOS signal, and flags. The Coast Guard will expect you to carry at least the minimum quantity. Be aware that all pyrotechnic signaling devices need to be replaced periodically, because they have expiration dates of 42 months from the date of manufacture. Keep the old ones as spares. The chances are they will work for some time after their expiration date if they have been stored in a watertight container. If you decide to dispose of pyrotechnic devices, note that they are extremely hazardous, flammable waste. Give them to the local fire or police department, the Coast Guard Auxiliary, or a similar organization for proper disposal.

The emergency signals are characterized as day and night signals: a handheld or floating smoke flare, signaling mirrors and flags, are daytime signals, whereas meteor and parachute flares (either handheld or fired from a flare launcher) and handheld red flares are night signals. The USCG minimum is three handheld red flares or one handheld red flare and two parachute flares or one handheld orange smoke flare, two floating orange smoke flares and one electric distress signal. The best way to outfit your boat is to buy one of the kits available at any good chandlery. The kit will come in a waterproof container and should be stored in a secure yet easily accessible place. As with fire extinguishers, the bare minimum required by law is just that. A few additional flares are cheap insurance.

Flare launchers come in two sizes, 12 gauge and 25 millimeter. Flares from a 25 mm launcher are the more visible by far. The money saved with 12-gauge flares will seem a poor bargain if you ever need them. You can purchase an adapter that will allow you to use 12-gauge flares in a 25 mm launcher, thus making use of existing flares if you change launchers.

The brightest flares, both meteor and parachute, are the SOLAS (Safety Of Life At Sea) flares. They are sold individually and do not use a launcher. A SOLAS parachute flare lasts for 40 seconds, as opposed to 29 seconds for a 25 mm parachute flare.

You also can signal distress by hand. Hold your arms out to each side and slowly raise and lower them. The distress flag, at least three feet square, is orange with a red circle and a black square in the center.

Flares must be used with care. They are hot and flammable, and can injure you or damage the boat. Treat flare launchers as you would a firearm and never point it at anyone. Handheld flares should be held at arm's length, pointing downwind and over the side to avoid dripping molten material onto the boat. If you have leather gloves, put them on before igniting the flare. Launch meteor and parachute flares at an angle of 60 degrees above the horizon in calm air and closer to vertical as the wind increases. Don't fire them straight up—what goes up must come down! Turn your head at the moment you fire them.

Floating smoke flares are excellent day signals for aircraft. They produce dense, orange smoke, yet will not ignite fuel that may be floating on the water. Put them in the water downwind of your boat or life raft.

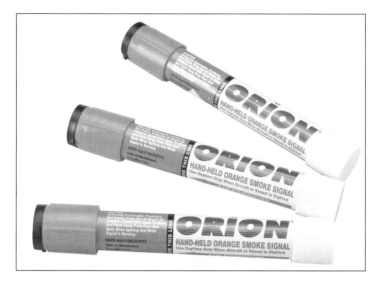

The handheld red safety flares above meet USCG minimum safety requirements, as long as at least three are onboard. Search and rescue experts recommend carrying at least six.

Practice is vital, but you can't just fire a flare or light a handheld flare any time you feel the need to practice, no matter what the conditions. That is the equivalent of setting off a false alarm and is a punishable offense. As with fire extinguishers, the US Power Squadrons or the Coast Guard Auxiliary occasionally has flare practice days. Attend one of these events to get the feel for the procedure.

Meteor flares shoot a flaming red ball into the air, like a larger version of a Roman candle. The flares go up to a height of 250 to 450 feet (depending on the type) and fall back into the sea, with a total time of less than seven seconds. A parachute flare sits in the sky much longer, between 29 and 40 seconds, again depending on the variety. Handheld red flares last two minutes and handheld smoke flares will produce smoke for one to three minutes, depending on the type. Floating smoke flares produce smoke for four minutes.

If you fire a meteor flare, shoot two, separated by 15 to 30 seconds. The first will get someone's attention, and the second will allow that person to take a bearing on your location.

Don't launch flares unless you think there is someone to see them. Regardless of how many you have on board, your supply is limited.

A signaling mirror is remarkably effective in daylight. To use it, put the mirror to your eye, look through the grid in the center, extend your other hand, and make a "V" with your fingers. Place the target between your two fingers and flash the sun's reflections between your two fingers, with the target in the middle. People will see intermittent flashes of light even at a distance of several miles.

Your radio is the best means of attracting attention in an emergency. Remember that a Mayday call is not to be done casually. It is only for situations with immediate and serious danger. Running out of fuel or being aground, when no danger to the boat or its passengers is present, does not warrant a Mayday call. Instead, use a Pan Pan, advising all listening of a situation that concerns the safety of your boat or other boats, or the safety of a person.

Your radio is preferable to your cell phone, even if you are in cell phone range. A cell phone call only goes to the number you are dialing, whereas everyone within range will hear a radio transmission. This is one time when you don't want a private communication.

Follow this specific formula to follow when sending a Mayday. Speak slowly and carefully, pronouncing each word. Transmit continuously until the Mayday message is delivered. Use channel 16 of your VHF radio or the emergency distress frequency 2182 kHz if you have a single-side-band (SSB) radio. All Coast Guard stations and all commercial vessels that have a SSB radio when underway monitor 2182 kHz. Because its range is greater, the chances of being heard are much higher. VHF is a line-of-sight frequency, but SSB signals can go over the horizon.

Mayday Call

"Mayday, mayday, mayday.
    "This is [your boat's name]." Repeat three times.
    "Mayday.
    "This is [boat name].
    "Our location is [give the coordinates of your position or your location in terms of direction and distance from a point on land]."

State the nature of your emergency: sinking, fire, life-threatening medical emergency, abandoning ship, etc.

State the kind of assistance needed: pumps, recovering crew from life raft, etc.

Conclude with any information that will help the rescuers find and assist you. That could include distinguishing features of your boat, the number of crew needing rescue, and so on.

If you do not get a response within about a minute, send the Mayday again. If, after several attempts on channel 16 you still get no response, try going to a channel where you have heard recent traffic or one you have used for a recent communication.

If you hear a Mayday, immediately clear the channel and cease any transmissions in progress. Do not answer it immediately, as the Coast Guard or a vessel closer to the emergency may be trying to answer. Listen, take notes if possible and, if there is no answer after the second call, respond to

the Mayday. As with the sending of a Mayday, there is a specific, internationally agreed-upon formula for response.

Responding to a Mayday

State (one time) the name of the vessel that sent the Mayday, and repeat "Mayday" three times.
    "This is [your vessel's name]." Repeat three times.
    "Received.
    "Mayday."

After this, give your location, your speed, and the esti-
mated time of arrival at the Mayday boat's location.
    Then, attempt to relay the Mayday to the Coast Guard or
other vessels that may be closer to the Mayday vessel. Follow this formula:

    "Mayday, mayday, mayday.
    "This is [your boat name]." Repeat three times.

Following this formula will make it obvious to the Coast
Guard or any other recipient of the relayed Mayday that
you are making a relay and are not the vessel in distress.
    Once you hear a Mayday, sending any messages on that
frequency is forbidden. If the Coast Guard becomes involved, they will announce radio silence with the words
"Seelonce Mayday." Radio silence will continue until notification by the Coast Guard or the rescuing authority, which
is provided in a set formula.

    "Mayday."
    "Hello all stations." This is repeated three times.

"This is [the station making the announcement]." The phrase will be repeated three times.

The time the transmission is being made will be stated.

The announcement will conclude with the words, "Seelonce Finay" or "Pru-Donce."

A Pan Pan message is often used by the Coast Guard to advise of a vessel that is overdue or missing or of a person overboard. A Pan Pan can either be an advisory or a request for assistance, and it begins with the words "Pan Pan," repeated three times, followed by the message.

The lowest category of what are termed "priority transmissions" is the "Securitay" message, usually used before announcements concerning navigational safety (such as the planned passage of a large vessel or the condition of an aid to navigation) or weather alerts.

If you are going offshore or making extended coastal cruises, a life raft is an important part of your emergency equipment. Life rafts come in a wide variety of sizes, types, and prices. They are available in either a hard case or a soft valise, each with its own advantages and disadvantages. Seek out a dealer who specializes in their sale and servicing for advice on the life raft that suits your needs. Its use and deployment will be explained thoroughly by the dealer.

The basic advice on a life raft is never get into one unless it requires a step up. Stay with your boat until the headliner is wet. A boat is much easier for rescuers to see than any life raft. A life raft of any size or type is uncomfortable, wet, cramped, and only tolerable if there are literally no alternatives.

CHAPTER 15

OVERBOARD

One rule that can be said to be the number one rule of boating is, "Stay on the boat." It is considered very bad form to return to the dock with fewer people in your boat than when you left. The good news is that avoiding losing someone over the side is not difficult.

Despite your best intentions, however, people do sometimes fall overboard. That is why you have lifejackets on board, and why people wear them. You or your passengers can end up in the water by falling over the side, or if the boat capsizes. Because neither of these events are planned, putting on your lifejacket before you need it is always the best idea.

Sailors on sailboats are tied to their boat during bad weather and at night, but they have to spend more time on deck (as opposed to being in the cockpit) than anyone on a powerboat, especially when the weather is bad. When things get nasty, put passengers in the cockpit or, below into the cabin. A word of warning: anyone prone to getting seasick may not be able to tolerate the movement when the boat is being tossed around, so the cockpit may be the only choice. Everyone should keep their hands on the rails or handholds, found on almost all boats. and of course all passengers should have their lifejackets on and firmly fastened. That includes the skipper.

Part of the pre-trip briefing you have with your passengers must include what to do if anyone goes overboard. The first thing is to shout out "Man overboard." Then throw cushions or lifejackets or anything handy to the victim to help him stay afloat. Throw a lot of them, to help mark the spot where the incident happened and make it easier to find the man overboard (MOB). These floating objects will include what the Coast Guard likes to call Type IV throwable devices, but to the rest of us they look like cushions with a strap on each side.

If there is another person on board, have that person do nothing else but point to the victim. The pointer extends his hand and keeps it pointed directly at the MOB. It is very easy to lose sight of someone in the water because all you can see is that person's head. The MOB will frequently be hidden from view, often obscured by waves.

If you're alone on the boat, keep your eyes on the MOB. It is all too easy for a person to disappear from view in any kind of a seaway.

Immediately shut down the throttle, hit the "MOB" button on your GPS, make a 180-degree U-turn as soon as it is safe to do so, and begin to maneuver back to the MOB. The MOB button enters your position at that instant and will help you get back to the place where the person went over. If he went over while you were on a plane and doing 40 knots, he will be a good distance away from the boat. At 40 knots, your boat travels 67 feet in one second.

After the turn, be aware that a 180-degree turn to the right will put your previous track to your right. Look for the center of your wake, the trail of small bubbles churned by the prop, and put your bow directly over it.

While you are getting to the MOB, prepare for getting him back on board. That may involve lowering the board-

MOB Recovery and Retrieval Using Lifesling

1 Shout "man overboard" and throw flotation devices, including cushions and non-attached life ring (if available). Assign one crewmember to point continually at the MOB using an outstretched arm.

2 Turn upwind, adjusting throttle as needed to negotiate seaway.

3 Throw LifeSling to MOB, circle or pass nearby (upwind from MOB) to get LifeSling to MOB. (The line attaching the LifeSling to the boat is made of polypropylene and floats.)

4 With forward motion ceased, cut power to engines. Ensure that props are not running.

5 Pull MOB to leeward side of boat.

6 The MOB can be brought aboard by attaching line from the davit or boom used to launch the tender. A swim step with a boarding ladder can also be used for MOB recovery. BE CAREFUL THAT THE BOAT'S MOTION DOESN'T INJURE MOB.

7 If the MOB is unconscious, you may have to put crew in water to assist with rescue. Crew member should wear inflated lifejacket and be attached to boat with spare line.

ing ladder or preparing a length of floating line with a loop in it. If you have a LifeSling, get ready to throw it to the MOB. Come alongside the MOB with him upwind of you so the boat doesn't drift over him. Position the boat so that the MOB is at the lowest part of the boat, usually the stern, the swim platform, or the boarding ladder.

The boarding ladder can present its own hazards if the boat is moving heavily in the waves. It will be plunging up and down and can strike the MOB. Try to time the MOB getting on the ladder with its movement.

As soon as you are near, stop the engine and disengage the prop by putting the transmission in neutral. A rotating prop can inflict deadly injuries in a split second. If the rescue has taken any time, and especially if the water is cold, the MOB may be unable to offer any assistance in his recovery. He may also have been injured, either in the course of going overboard or while in the water.

If the recovery is going to take more than a few seconds, get on the radio and inform the Coast Guard with a Pan-Pan call (see Chapter 14) that you have an MOB. Give your location, boat name, and number of people in the water. Inform them that you are undertaking the rescue and that you will keep them up to date on progress. Tell them early; you don't want to wait until things have deteriorated and you need to mount a full-scale search. Of course, as soon as the MOB is safely back onboard, make another call to cancel the alert.

Do not allow anyone to jump in to help. You will then have two people you need to get out of the water. If there is no other alternative and you absolutely must have help in the water, put a lifejacket on the person and tie him or her to the boat.

A swim platform, if you have one, is an ideal location to recover the MOB. Unfortunately, it is also next to the propeller, so make sure that the prop is motionless. If the engine is running, someone could bump into the transmission lever and engage the prop, so shut off the engine.

Throw a line with a loop in it to the MOB as soon as you are near. Use polypropylene line so that it floats. A waterski tow line will work, although the loop in the end may not be big enough for the MOB to put around his chest. A Life-Sling will have a floating line attached to it and is strong enough to lift the MOB, but be aware that you will be lifting his entire weight plus the water in his clothes and shoes. You can get a block and tackle rig to go with that LifeSling to make the job easier. But, it requires having an attachment point that may be hard to find on a small boat.

If you put someone on the swim platform to help the MOB out of the water, tie him to the boat. Again, you don't want two people in the water. Be careful to not let everyone crowd against the rail. All that weight could tip the boat and a wave could break over the gunwale or transom.

Once he's back on board, get the MOB out of his wet clothes. If he's cold, wrap him in dry blankets or in a sleeping bag. Putting someone next to him will help get warmth to his body, and if you have a hot water bottle, place it on his neck, by his chest, or in the groin area. Cold water can induce hypothermia in a matter of minutes. Water at 40 degrees Fahrenheit, which is found in much of our country's coastal waters, can chill an immersed person to unconsciousness in 15 minutes.

Take the person's vital signs. Make sure the airway is clear and the person can breathe easily. Check the pulse and respiration, which may be weak. An oral thermometer will not give an accurate reading of core body temperature. A rectal thermometer is the only accurate method of determining true body temperature.

If the person is mildly chilled, with a core temperature

between 93 and 97 degrees, he will be shivering, with cold hands and feet, but lucid and able to help himself. He will be clumsy, lack dexterity, and feel pain from the cold. He can be given warm, sweet drinks and allowed to exercise to regain body heat. Do not supply anything alcoholic to drink. Hot water bottles and a dry, warm blanket or sleeping bag will speed recovery.

With a core temperature between 90 and 93 degrees, shivering may cease. Do not offer anything to drink until the person can swallow and has warmed up. Apply gentle warmth as noted above.

If you suspect the person is more severely hypothermic, with a core temperature below 90 degrees, do not give him anything hot to drink. Do not allow the person to get up, walk, or exercise. Don't rub the skin. Improper warming of a hypothermia victim can send chilled blood from the extremities into the body's core, inducing what is known as After-Drop and reducing the temperature of the body's core even further.

Put the person in a bunk with feet elevated and apply gentle warmth, but don't try to raise the temperature too quickly. Persons with this level of hypothermia need medical care. Do not begin cardio-pulmonary resuscitation (CPR) unless the heart and breathing have stopped.

If any of these symptoms exist, or you suspect the overboard victim of being anything other than wet and embarrassed, get to medical care as soon as possible. One of the symptoms of hypothermia is the inability to think clearly. You can't always believe the standard assurance that "I'm fine."

Experiences with losing a man overboard are all too typical. Someone goes over the side when you least expect it; he isn't wearing a lifejacket, and suddenly you have an

Coast Guard regulations require all children under 13 to wear an approved life-jacket when underway.

emergency on your hands. Without a lifejacket, dunked suddenly into the water, and in shock over the rapid turn of events, even an experienced swimmer can have difficulty staying afloat.

Part of the lesson here is the one that is repeated end-lessly in all boating courses and advisories. Hold on, all the time. Wear your lifejacket. New developments in lifejackets now include lightweight inflatable vests that inflate auto-matically when they get wet. They are light, and comfort-able, and you can wear them all day, even without a shirt if it's a hot day. These inflatable vests have a collar that will turn even an unconscious person right-side up so he can breathe. Their official USCG nomenclature is "Type V with type III (or type II) performance." They are the easiest to use of all the various types of lifejackets. A smaller version uses a belt-pack inflatable that looks like a nylon-webbing belt with a small package attached. These are recommended only for adults who are good swimmers, because you have to put the inflated bladder over your head after it is inflated. The harness variety is ready to go as soon as it inflates, which only takes a second or two. Both the harness and the belt-pack are available with automatic inflating devices that sense being in the water and inflate immediately. The automatic versions have a manual override feature allowing you to pull the ripcord and inflate it yourself.

Note that if you are boarded by the Coast Guard for a lifejacket count, the number of lifejackets has to equal or exceed the number of people onboard.

Don't forget your children. Inflatables are not USCG-approved for wear by children under the age of 16. Coast Guard regulations require all children under the age of 13 to wear an approved, well-fitted lifejacket at all times when underway unless they are in an enclosed cabin or below decks.

It's important for your children to feel comfortable with their lifejacket, and the easiest way to do this is for them to put it on and get in the water. Show them how to adjust it and help them get the fit right so it doesn't come up over their head. Once they see how secure it feels to have it on and be able to effortlessly float in the water, they will be converted. Give them a good example and have the grownups wear theirs also.

APPENDIX

VHF Radio: Operation and Protocol

Index

VHF RADIO: OPERATION AND PROTOCOL

VHF, or Very High Frequency, radios are the primary means of communication for boats operating near the coast and for land-based maritime stations communicating with boats or other land stations. Cell phones may be convenient when boating, but VHF radios have the ability to do what no cell phone can do: broadcast. Whereas cell phones can only make calls from point A to point B, VHF radios can broadcast a message to every station within listening range. It is this broadcasting ability that makes VHF radios so important and will likely prevent cell phones from supplanting them as the primary means of marine communications.

Unlike cell phones, which use third-party towers to receive a signal and transmit a call, VHF radios transmit and receive line-of-sight signals directly to and from each other. There is no service area *per se*, as reception depends upon proximity to the receiving or transmitting station. As a result, land masses, large structures, the curvature of the earth and any other obstruction to your line of sight will block the VHF signal.

Before going much farther, it's important to clarify some definitions. A *station* refers to a radio that is being operated by a boat or an organization on land, such as a bridge controller. *Traffic* means any current conversation taking place on a VHF channel. VHF radios can only receive one signal at a time and will hear the strongest signal that is transmitted. If multiple stations are transmitting simultaneously on the same frequency, you will only hear the transmission from the strongest signal. Signal strength is controlled by both distance between stations and the power at which a station is broadcasting. All VHF radios can be set to transmit at 1 watt. Handheld VHFs are limited to a transmit power of 6 watts, and fixed-mount VHFs to 25 watts, on the high end. On most radios, you can switch between high and low power by the appropriately labeled buttons or one labeled H/L. In general, it is best to try reaching your party on 1 watt before trying on high power, because it will minimize the amount of interference from other stations.

Because VHF radios work via line-of-sight, antenna installation is paramount, and is in fact the most important variable affecting the range of your VHF. Antennas make sure that the signal transmitted from your radio is radiated in the correct direction. If using a handheld VHF, you should stand on a high point on the deck, away from obvious obstructions and make sure the antenna is pointing straight up, as the signal will be transmitted perpendicular to the antenna. Fixed-mount radios should be paired with 6dB or 9dB antennas as they produce the greatest range. Sailboards can use 3dB antennas because they take into account a sailboat's tendency to heel over and broadcast at a greater angle. However, they have a lesser range.

Also unlike cell phones, VHF radios can only transmit or receive at any given moment. There's no interrupting or multitasking conversations on a VHF. Fixed-mount VHF radios have a microphone on a cord attached to the main radio. Handheld VHFs have the mike built into the radio itself. In both cases, there is a transmit button beside the mike. When the radio is turned on, it will be continuously receiving, or listening, until the transmit button is depressed. Alternatively, when transmitting, you will not be able to hear any other traffic.

As a result of a VHF radio's ability to hear only one station at a time and its inability to transmit and receive signals simultaneously, it can take some practice to feel comfortable using the radio. When transmitting, you should wait 30 seconds to a minute to make sure no one else is using the frequency. Remember that because a radio can only hear one station at a time, your intended recipient may not be able to hear you, or you may interfere with another station if you broadcast simultaneously. If you haven't heard anything, depress the transmit button fully. Then speak slowly and clearly into the mike. Keep your message succinct, and release the transmit button when you're finished. If you don't release the transmit button, not only will you not be able to hear any response to your call, but you will also continue to transmit the background noise and conversation from your boat. Whoever you are, you don't want to be *that guy*.

Most radios have a gain knob near the volume knob. To ensure clearest reception, turn the gain knob until you hear total static. Then back it off until the static stops.

Channels and Frequencies

VHF radios use the FM (Frequency Modulated) band. Every channel corresponds to a different frequency, and higher channels have higher frequencies. Though it is not important to know the actual frequencies, it is important to know the purposes of all the different channels. After all, a buddy boat can be a quarter mile away, hailing you on channel 9, but if you are on 68, you'll never hear him. VHF radios broadcast to all stations within range that are listening *on the specific channel being used for transmission.*

Commercial operations rely on VHF radios to communicate important information. They cannot deal with recreational conversations. Emergency channels need to be kept clear for priority traffic. Marinas monitor specific channels so that they can correspond with boats moving about their docks. In order to keep the airwaves from being a jumble of conversations interfering with each other, VHF channels have assigned purposes, listed below. The bold channels are the ones you're most likely to use. A common practice is to monitor channels 9, 16, 13 if you are in a commercial harbor, and one of the non-commercial channels, such as 72, that you have pre-arranged with friends.

VHF Channels and Their Use

01A	Port Operations and Commercial traffic. Available only in New Orleans/Lower Mississippi area.
05A	Port Operations in the Houston, New Orleans and Seattle areas.
6	Intership Safety (Safety traffic between ships)
07A	Commercial traffic
8	Commercial traffic between ships (no shore stations)
9	Hailing for commercial and non-commercial traffic. Use this channel to call another boat, and then switch to a non-commercial working channel.
10	Commercial traffic
11	Commercial traffic

12	Port Operations traffic
13	Intership Navigation Safety. In major harbors, cargo ships, tug boats, cruise ships and other large vessel broadcast their maneuvers on channel 13. Because their ability to maneuver is limited by the generally tight space of a harbor, they broadcast their intentions to avoid confusion and possible collisions. They will also hail ships on channel 13 as opposed to 9 or 16. If boating in a major harbor, you should monitor channel 13 so you are aware of the major movements in the harbor, and so that a large ship can hail you if necessary. If unsure about a ship's intentions, you can hail it on 13; sometimes large ships don't even monitor 16 or 9.
14	Port Operations
16	International Distress, Safety and Calling. All ships that are required to carry a radio and most coastal stations maintain a listening watch on channel 16. If in an emergency, broadcast message on channel 16. If able, always monitor channel 16. Channel 16 can be used to hail another boat if you have failed to make contact on other hailing channels, such as 9.
17	State Control
18A	Commercial traffic
19A	Commercial traffic
20	Port Operations
20A	Port Operations
21A	U.S. Coast Guard only
22A	Coast Guard Liaison and Maritime Safety Information Broadcasts. Broadcasts are first announced on channel 16, then the actual broadcast occurs on 22A. For example, on channel 16, Coast

Guard might announce that it will broadcast latest weather on 22A. If you switch to 22A, you will then hear the weather forecast.

23A	Public Correspondence (Marine Operator)
25	Public Correspondence (Marine Operator)
26	Public Correspondence (Marine Operator)
27	Public Correspondence (Marine Operator)
28	Public Correspondence (Marine Operator)
63A	Port Operations and Commercial. Available only in New Orleans/Lower Mississippi area.
65A	Port Operations
66A	Port Operations
67	Commercial. Used for bridge-to-bridge communications in lower Mississippi only.
68	Non-Commercial traffic ("working channel")
69	Non-Commercial traffic
70	Digital Selective Calling (voice communications not allowed)
71	Non-Commercial traffic
72	Non-Commercial (Intership only) traffic
73	Port Operations traffic
74	Port Operations traffic
77	Port Operations (Intership only) traffic
78A	Non-Commercial traffic
79A	Commercial traffic. Non-Commercial in Great Lakes only
80A	Commercial traffic. Non-Commercial in Great Lakes only
81A	U.S. Government only - Environmental protection operations
82A	U.S. Government only
83A	U.S. Coast Guard only
84	Public Correspondence (Marine Operator)
85	Public Correspondence (Marine Operator)

86	Public Correspondence (Marine Operator)
87	Automatic Identification System duplex repeater
88A	Commercial, Intership traffic only.

Most radios have the ability to monitor multiple channels, and you can choose which channels to monitor. These radios scroll through the chosen channels and pause on one if there is any traffic. In this way, you can always monitor 16 for priority traffic while listening for your friends on a non-commercial channel. If your VHF radio does not have the ability to monitor multiple channels, you should monitor channel 16, and switch to one of the non-commercial channels to talk with friends. If your radio is equipped with the scroll feature and you hear something that you need to respond to, be sure that you switch your radio to the correct channel to broadcast, otherwise, you might broadcast on whichever channel your radio happens to be scrolling through when you pick up the mike.

Digital Selective Calling

Digital Selective Calling (DSC) is a new technology that is revolutionizing maritime radios. All new VHF radio models are DSC-equipped. DSC makes a VHF radio able to work more like a telephone in addition to its normal VHF capabilities. It allows boaters to send a digital call directly to another DSC-equipped vessel or shore station, much like a text message on a cell phone. Channel 70 has been set aside as the VHF/DSC digital call channel. Once the DSC call has been confirmed, both parties switch to a working voice channel.

In order for DSC-equipped VHF radios to function properly, they must first be programmed with the boat's unique maritime ID number, called a Maritime Mobile Service Identity (MMSI) number. Boats under 65 feet can contact BoatUS or MariTEL to get an MMSI number. This MMSI number will act as your maritime phone number. The radio must also be connected to the ship's GPS. That way, in case of an emergency, a DSC distress call will automatically tell the Coast Guard your position and information about the type and size of the boat and contact information for the boat owner. However, it is important to note that at present not all USCG stations are equipped with DSC, though they are moving in that direction. Therefore, a distress call on DSC will only be heard by other DSC-equipped vessels and should be followed immediately by a voice distress call.

The red "Distress" button on the front of DSC-equipped VHF radios automatically sends a DSC distress message on channel 70.

In addition to DSC's safety features, if you have your radio programmed with the MMSI number of another boat, you can selectively hail just that vessel on DSC channel 70 and then switch to an appropriate voice channel. However, be aware that while you can selectively call your desired vessel, the voice communications take place on a standard VHF channel and are broadcast to everyone in range listening on that station.

Non-emergency Protocols

The VHF radio's broadcast ability is a double-edged sword. With the exception of DSC operations, all communications via VHF are broadcast to all stations within listening range. This means that while your emergency message will be heard by the maximum number of people ready to assist, your casual chat about the relative fullness of the fish hold and the beer cooler can also be heard all around. As a result, it is important to know and follow proper radio protocol. Not only do you want to avoid operating on emergency channels, preventing true emergency traffic, you don't want to sound like an idiot for all the world to hear.

Channel 16 should be used for hailing and emergencies only, and 9 should be used for hailing. Once you reach your desired party, you should switch to a non-commercial working channel (listed above). In many areas, if casual conversations persist on channel 16 (and sometimes 9) the Coast Guard will break in and remind parties of this, and that they must switch to a working channel.

Also, brevity is highly valued in VHF communications and most conversations should be kept under a few minutes. Because there are a limited number of working channels that must be shared by all of the boating traffic, you don't want to hog a channel with lengthy discussions about cocktail plans or the like. Also, reception is often less than crystal clear, and it is difficult to understand what someone else is saying. Therefore, there is a specific radio terminology used to aid efficient, clear radio communications:

Roger means "I understand what you said". It does not imply that you either agree or disagree

Affirmative means "yes". "Yes", "uh-huh" and "yep" are difficult to understand over the radio.

Negative means "no".

Niner is used for the number "nine" because it is very easy to confuse "nine" for other words.

Over means you are finished speaking and it is now the other person's turn to speak.

Out means that the conversation is finished and you are returning to a hailing station. Note that you never say, "over and out" only one or the other.

Negative copy means that you did not understand what the other station said and they should repeat their transmission.

In addition to the special terminology, there is a specific protocol you should follow when hailing another boat. Note that the entire transmission should take less than 30 seconds on the hailing channel:

First listen on a hailing channel (9 or 16) to make sure no one else is using it.

Depress the transmit button and say the name of the boat you are hailing three times followed by the name of your boat:

Knot Now, Knot Now, Knot Now this is Early Retirement over.

Release the transmit button and listen for *Knot Now*'s response. If they do not respond, wait a minute before trying again. If they do respond, they should say:

Early Retirement this is Knot Now, switch and answer on 7-2, over

Note that instead of saying "seventy-two" you say the digits of the number "seven two".

Your response:

Roger Knot Now, switching 7-2, over

If *Knot Now* did not suggest a channel to switch to, follow the same format and choose a non-commercial working channel from the list above.

When finished with your conversation on channel 72,

say "out" and indicate which channel you are switching back to:

This is Early Retirement out, switching back to 1-6 and niner

With a little practice, and a little time spent with your specific radio's owner's manual, you will soon be using your VHF radio with ease, and sounding like an old pro.

INDEX